About This Book

Many teachers are overwhelmed with the task of meeting the individual needs of each of their students. It is very important to implement activities that reach all of the different learning modalities. Often, books offer many teaching ideas, but they fail to help teachers implement them. *Phonics: Games & Learning Activities* not only offers the lesson ideas but also the ready-to-use materials to use with the lessons. These activities have been tried and tested in actual classrooms, and they have been found to be motivating, enjoyable, and all-around successful. They are designed to make your life easier because they require very little preparation time. Almost all of the activities can be used at learning centers or as whole-class activities.

Preparation Suggestions

1. Copy all of the activity materials onto heavy cardstock and laminate them. This will give the materials years of durability. Cardstock is available at just about any office supply store, and it is worth the investment.

2. Prepare a writing connection to go along with each activity. This will help to reinforce the featured skill, and it will also help the students to give more meaning to their writing.

3. Make extra copies of each game or activity. These can be sent home with those students who might need more practice with specific skills.

4. Tape game boards together on the backsides, not the front, because the tape is likely to yellow with age. Also, paste game boards onto pieces of heavy poster board and then laminate them.

5. The learning games in this book can be used as interesting and motivating free-choice activities, or they can be used with teacher supervision after discussions of the emphasized skills.

6. Most importantly, be sure to model each game or activity several times. As you explain how to use each activity, include auditory examples of saying the words out loud, blending out loud, etc.

Final "E" Book

Skills: adding the final "e"
long vowel sounds

Materials

- copies of pages 5–14 for each student
- scissors for each student
- a stapler and staples

Preparation

Copy one Final "E" Book for each student. (**Note:** Be sure to run the copies back-to-back so that the letter "e" side can be folded over to make the new word.) Pair pages as follows: 5 and 6, 7 and 8, 9 and 10, 11 and 12, 13 and 14.

Procedure

1. Ask the students to cut out the pages of their books. Encourage them to cut carefully along the dotted lines, so as not to cut off any of the pictures or letters.
2. Help the students staple their books together along the left sides.
3. Next, tell the students to fold tab down along the solid line on each page. When a page is folded, the original picture will be covered and the letter "e" will be added to the word. See the example below.

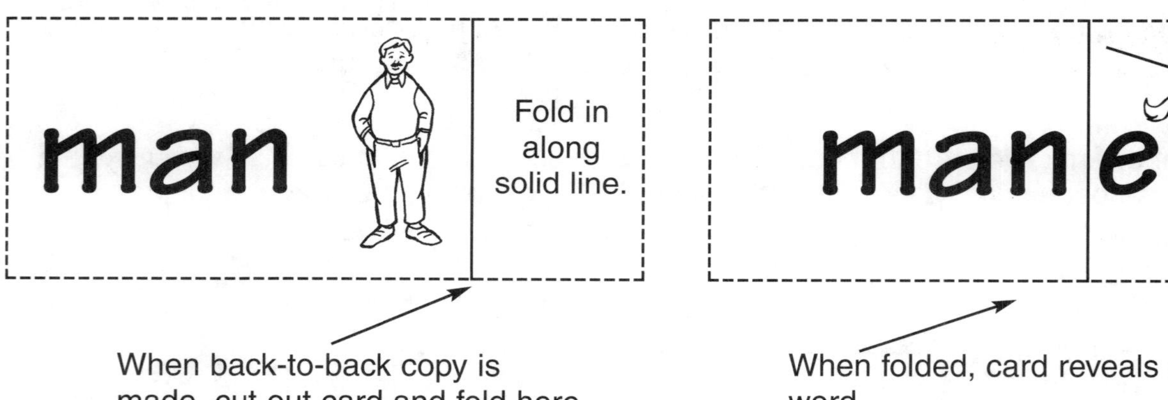

4. To use their books, the students first say the word on a page without the final "e." They then add the final "e" to the word and say the new word.

Writing Connections

- ✏ Tell the students to choose four or more words from their books. Have them each write a sentence which uses one of the words without the final "e." Ask them to write another sentence, using the word with the final "e." This activity reinforces the different meanings of words with and without the final "e."
- ✏ Ask the students to each choose four or more words and use them in a story.

Final "E" Book (cont.)

can 

Fold in along solid line.

cap 

Fold in along solid line.

mop 

Fold in along solid line.

Final "E" Book (cont.)

e

e

e

Final "E" Book (cont.)

wok 	Fold in along solid line.
man 	Fold in along solid line.
pin 	Fold in along solid line.

Final "E" Book (cont.)

e

e

e

Final "E" Book (cont.)

tub 

Fold in along solid line.

not 

Fold in along solid line.

Fold in along solid line.

Final "E" Book (cont.)

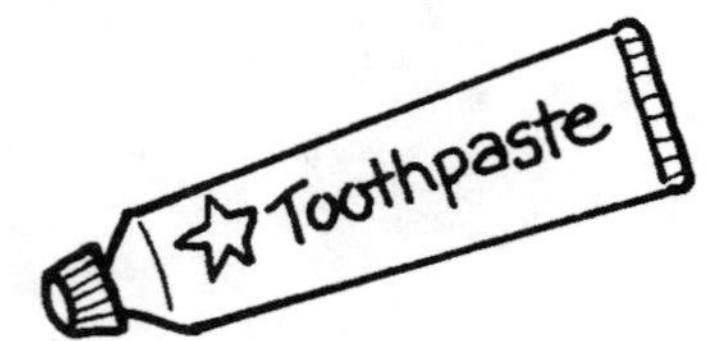

e

e

Final "E" Book (cont.)

grad 

Fold in along solid line.

rod 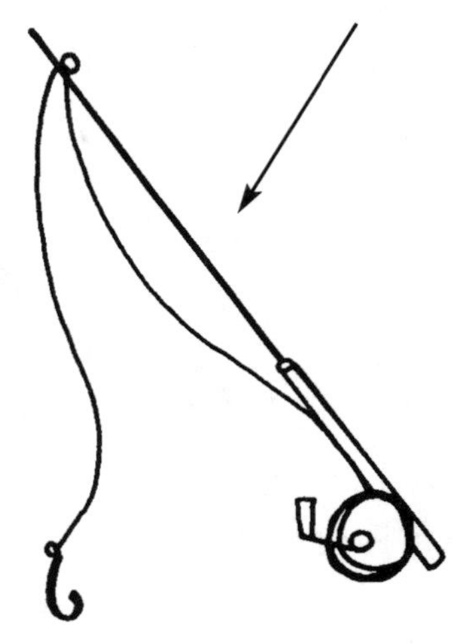

Fold in along solid line.

pan 

Fold in along solid line.

Final "E" Book (cont.)

e

e

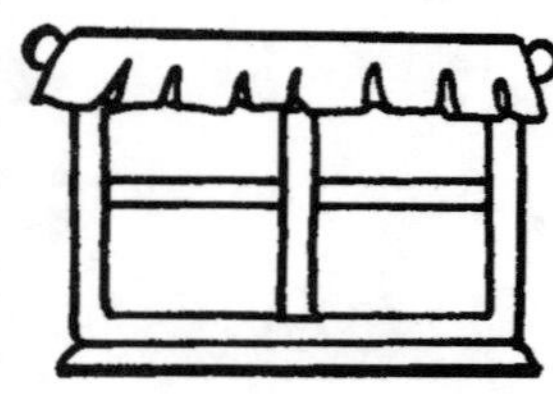

e

Final "E" Book (cont.)

plan 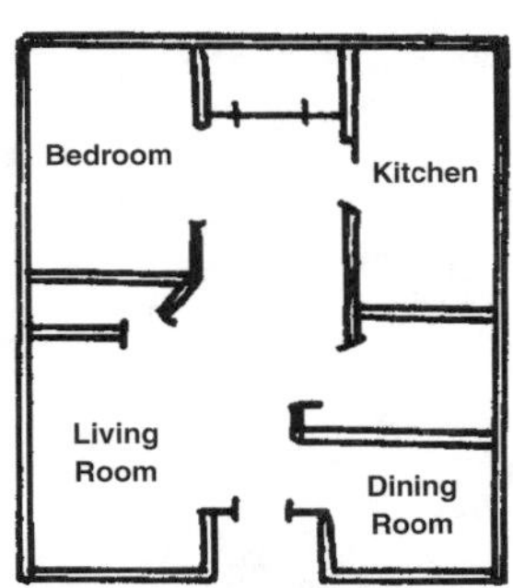	**Fold in along solid line.**
rat 	**Fold in along solid line.**
cut 	**Fold in along solid line.**

Final "E" Book (cont.)

e

e

e

Magic "E" Adventure

Skills: adding the final "e"

vowel and consonant discrimination

Materials

- copies of pages 16–18 for each pair or group
- any small items which could be used as game pieces (beans, buttons, etc.)
- dice
- tape
- scissors
- crayons or markers
- poster board

Preparation

1. Copy the Magic "E" Adventure game (pages 17 and 18) onto heavy cardstock. (Make enough game boards for every two to four players.)
2. To assemble a game board, cut page 17 along the the dashed line, and line it up on the solid line where indicated on page 18. Tape the two pages together on the back.
3. Color the "Start" square with a bright color. Color the rest of the squares, if you desire.
4. You may want to back the game with poster board and laminate it for durability.

Procedure *(2–4 players)*

1. Discuss how the letter "e" sometimes changes the sound and meaning of a word when it is placed at the end of a word. Cite some examples.
2. Hand out all of the game materials to each pair or group.
3. Read and discuss the directions (page 16) with the students.
4. Allow each pair or group a couple of practice plays before beginning the game.
5. Answer any questions.
6. Begin playing the game.

Variation

Require the players to also say the pattern of each word, for example, VCE, cute, and VC, cut. (V = vowel; C = consonant; E = silent/final "e")

Magic "E" Adventure (cont.)

How to Play

The object of the game is to be the first player to land on the Isle of Magic "E".

1. Roll the dice to see who goes first. The player with the highest number starts.
2. Each player moves his or her marker the number rolled on the dice.
3. When a player lands on a word, he or she must read the word out loud, then cover up the final "e" and read it out loud again (for example, "cute" and "cut").
4. If a player does not read the two words correctly (and in the correct order), the player must move his or her marker back to where it was at the beginning of the play. The other players will determine if the words have been read correctly.
5. It is all right to have more than one marker on a space.
6. To land on the Isle of Magic "E," a player must roll the exact number on the dice.
7. The first player to land on the Isle of Magic "E" wins the game.

Magic "E" Adventure (cont.)

Start	ride	tube	A mermaid needs help. Go back one space.
			rode
			pine
A shark attacks you. Go back two spaces.			A sea monster is in your way. Go back two spaces.
robe		bite	hide
cube		cape	

Cut along the dotted line.

Magic "E" Adventure (cont.)

pale	fate	made	pane
ripe	ISLE OF MAGIC "E"		Large waves push you forward. Take another turn.
site			hope
cute		tape	There is a shipwreck in the coral reef. Go back three spaces.
woke		dime	rate

Tape the dotted line on page 17 to this line.

Sound Bingo

Skills: discriminating digraph and diphthong sounds

position of blend and diphthong sounds

Materials

- copies of pages 20–43
- small items, such as beans or buttons, which could be used as game pieces (about 20 per student)
- scissors

Preparation

1. Choose which bingo game you would like your students to play. Pages 20–32 focus on digraphs, while pages 33–43 focus on both digraphs and diphthongs. (**Note:** If you choose to play the more advanced version of this game, you will need to make copies of the word cards on pages 30–32 and page 43.)
2. Copy one set of bingo cards for ten students or two sets for 20 students.
3. Copy the word cards onto heavy cardstock and cut them out.
4. You may wish to laminate all the cards so that they last longer.

Procedure *(10–20 players)*

1. Each student covers his or her Free Space with a marker.
2. The teacher reads a word card and calls out the word.
3. The students must listen carefully to the word and discriminate whether the word has a *ch, sh*, or *th* sound (or an *aw/au*, *ow/ou*, or *oi/oy* sound if they are playing the more challenging version). They must decide if the sound is at the beginning (B), middle (M), or end (E) of the word.
4. The students place their markers on the appropriate squares. For example, if the word was "chin", they would look for a box with the "ch" sound and a "B" since the sound is at the beginning of the word.
5. When a student places five markers in a row either horizontally, vertically, or diagonally, he or she should call out "Bingo." The student must then give a word for each box in the winning bingo row. These words may be the ones that were called or the students own words can be used as long as they fit the criteria of the boxes correctly.

Variations

1. If the cards have been laminated, the students may be asked to write the called words in crayon in each box instead of using place markers. The words can be wiped away after each round.
2. Instead of playing for five in a row, play "Blackout." In this game the winner is the person who completely covers a card with game pieces first.

Sound Bingo (cont.)

Digraphs—th, sh, ch

sh B	ch E	sh B	th B	sh E
th B	sh M	ch M	sh E	th M
sh E	th E	Free Space	th B	ch M
th B	sh B	ch M	sh B	th E
sh E	sh M	sh M	ch M	ch B

Sound Bingo (cont.)

Digraphs—th, sh, ch

sh B	ch E	sh B	th B	sh E
ch B	sh M	ch M	sh E	th M
th E	th E	Free Space	ch B	ch M
sh B	ch B	th M	sh B	ch E
ch E	sh M	sh M	th M	sh B

Sound Bingo (cont.)

Digraphs—th, sh, ch

sh B	ch E	th B	ch B	sh E
th B	sh M	sh M	ch E	th M
sh E	th E	Free Space	th B	sh M
th B	ch B	th M	ch B	th E
ch E	sh M	ch M	th M	th B

Sound Bingo (cont.)

Digraphs—th, sh, ch

ch B	th E	sh B	ch B	sh E
th B	sh M	ch M	sh E	ch M
th E	th E	Free Space	th B	sh M
sh B	ch B	ch M	sh B	th E
ch E	sh M	sh M	th M	sh B

Sound Bingo (cont.)

Digraphs—th, sh, ch

sh B	th E	sh B	th B	ch E
th B	sh M	ch M	sh E	th M
sh E	th E	Free Space	th B	sh M
ch B	sh B	th M	ch B	th E
sh E	ch M	sh M	ch M	sh B

Sound Bingo (cont.)

Digraphs—th, sh, ch

sh B	**th** E	**sh** B	**ch** B	**sh** E
ch B	**ch** M	**th** M	**sh** E	**ch** M
th E	**sh** E	Free Space	**th** B	**th** M
sh B	**ch** B	**ch** M	**sh** B	**th** E
ch E	**th** M	**sh** M	**ch** M	**sh** B

Sound Bingo (cont.)

Digraphs—th, sh, ch

sh B	ch E	sh B	ch B	th E
th B	ch M	sh M	th E	ch M
ch E	sh E	Free Space	ch B	th M
th B	ch B	th M	sh B	th E
ch E	sh M	th M	ch M	sh B

Sound Bingo (cont.)

Digraphs—th, sh, ch

th B	sh E	ch B	th B	th E
sh B	th M	ch M	th E	ch M
sh E	th E	Free Space	ch B	sh M
ch B	sh B	ch M	th B	th E
th E	sh M	ch M	sh M	ch B

Sound Bingo (cont.)

Digraphs—th, sh, ch

th B	th E	ch B	sh B	th E
ch B	ch M	th M	ch E	ch M
ch E	th E	Free Space	th B	sh M
ch B	sh B	th M	sh B	th E
th E	ch M	sh M	ch M	sh B

Sound Bingo (cont.)

Digraphs—th, sh, ch

ch B	th E	sh B	ch B	th E
ch B	ch M	th M	th E	ch M
sh E	sh E	Free Space	th B	sh M
ch B	th B	ch M	sh B	th E
th E	sh M	th M	ch M	ch B

Sound Bingo (cont.)

Word Cards—th

that	with	toothbrush
thin	both	bathtub
thud	bath	athlete
this	math	gothic
thing	path	northern
throb	tooth	pathway
thick	south	toothpaste
think	sixth	southern
third	broth	youthful

Sound Bingo (cont.)

Word Cards—sh

shut	crash	flushing
ship	wash	crashing
shop	dish	bashful
short	fish	dishes
shark	wish	ashes
shunt	flash	washes
shell	gash	crushes
shed	cash	bushes
sham	finish	lashes

Sound Bingo (cont.)

Word Cards—ch

chick	pinch	enchant
chat	watch	matches
chip	clench	branches
chum	much	riches
chop	such	richly
chin	bench	ranches
chair	bunch	lunches
child	crunch	drenched
chest	punch	porches

Sound Bingo (cont.)

Digraphs and Diphthongs

sh B	aw/au E	sh B	th B	sh E
ow/ou B	sh M	ch M	ow/ou E	oi/oy M
sh E	ch E	Free Space	th B	ch M
th B	th B	ch M	aw/au B	th E
oi/oy E	sh M	sh M	ch M	oi/oy B

Sound Bingo (cont.)

Digraphs and Diphthongs

sh B	oi/oy E	sh B	ow/ou B	sh E
ch B	sh M	ch M	aw/au E	th M
oi/oy E	ow/ou E	Free Space	ch B	ch M
sh B	oi/oy B	th M	sh B	ch E
ch E	sh M	sh M	th M	aw/au B

Sound Bingo (cont.)

Digraphs and Diphthongs

sh B	ch E	th B	ow/ou B	sh E
oi/oy B	sh M	sh M	aw/au E	th M
sh E	th E	Free Space	th B	sh M
th B	ch B	aw/au M	ch B	oi/oy E
ow/ou E	sh M	ch M	th M	th B

Sound Bingo (cont.)

Digraphs and Diphthongs

ow/ou B	th E	sh B	aw/au B	sh E
th B	sh M	ch M	sh E	ch M
th E	ow/ou E	Free Space	oi/oy B	sh M
sh B	ch B	aw/au M	sh B	th E
oi/oy E	sh M	sh M	th M	sh B

Sound Bingo (cont.)

Digraphs and Diphthongs

oi/oy B	th E	sh B	ch B	aw/au E
ch B	sh M	th M	sh E	th M
sh E	th E	Free Space	ow/ou B	sh M
aw/au B	sh B	th M	sh B	oi/oy E
sh E	ch M	ow/ou M	ch M	th B

Sound Bingo (cont.)

Digraphs and Diphthongs

sh B	th E	sh B	ch B	aw/au E
ch B	ch M	th M	oi/oy E	ch M
th E	ow/ou E	Free Space	th B	th M
ow/ou B	ch B	ch M	sh B	th E
ch E	aw/au M	sh M	oi/oy M	sh B

Sound Bingo (cont.)

Digraphs and Diphthongs

sh B	ch E	sh B	ch B	aw/au E
th B	oi/oy M	sh M	ow/ou E	ch M
ch E	sh E	Free Space	ch B	th M
ow/ou B	ch B	aw/au M	sh B	oi/oy E
ch E	sh M	th M	ch M	sh B

Sound Bingo (cont.)

Digraphs and Diphthongs

th B	sh E	ch B	th B	th E
oi/oy B	th M	ow/ou M	th E	aw/au M
sh E	th E	Free Space	ch B	sh M
ch B	sh B	ch M	ow/ou B	oi/oy E
aw/au E	sh M	ch M	sh M	ch B

Sound Bingo (cont.)

Digraphs and Diphthongs

th B	th E	ch B	ow/ou B	th E
ch B	aw/au M	th M	ch E	ch M
oi/oy E	th E	Free Space	th B	oi/oy M
ch B	sh B	th M	aw/au B	th E
ow/ou E	ch M	sh M	ch M	sh B

Sound Bingo (cont.)

Digraphs and Diphthongs

ch B	aw/au E	sh B	ch B	th E
ch B	ch M	oi/oy M	th E	ow/ou M
sh E	sh E	Free Space	th B	sh M
oi/oy B	th B	ch M	aw/au B	th E
ow/ou E	sh M	th M	ch M	ch B

Sound Bingo (cont.)

Word Cards—oi/oy, aw/au, ow/ou

oil	saw	house
broil	raw	out
joist	lawn	couch
voice	fawn	pout
coin	hawk	mouth
employ	awesome	how
royal	haul	owl
oyster	caught	frown
toy	pause	vow

Phonics Activity

Sound Search

Skill: discriminating digraph sounds

Materials

- copies of pages 45–48
- approximately 20 clothespins per table or center
- scissors
- crayons
- pencils

Preparation

1. Copy a set of the wheels (pages 45–47) for every group or center. (If you choose to do this activity in groups, limit the groups to three members each.)
2. Copy one answer sheet (page 48) for each student.
3. Carefully cut out the wheels. Color the pictures if you choose.
4. Laminate the wheels so that they can be used over and over again with minimal wear.

Procedures

1. Each student in the group, or at the center, will be given a wheel. The students will then study the wheels and search for the sounds that are in the wheel centers.
2. When a student finds a picture that has the sound of the letters in the center of the wheel, he or she will clip a clothespin to that picture.
3. After the student is done studying and marking (with clothespins) the wheel, he or she will use the answer sheet on page 48 to write each word that was found.
4. On their answer sheets, students may also draw pictures to go along with the words that they list.
5. After completing one column of the answer sheet, the students should then switch wheels and repeat the process until all three columns have been completed.

Writing Connections

- Ask the student to use three or four of the wheel words in a story. Encourage students to illustrate their stories.
- Challenge each student to use three or four of the wheel words in a single sentence. These sentences may then be illustrated.

Sound Search (cont.)

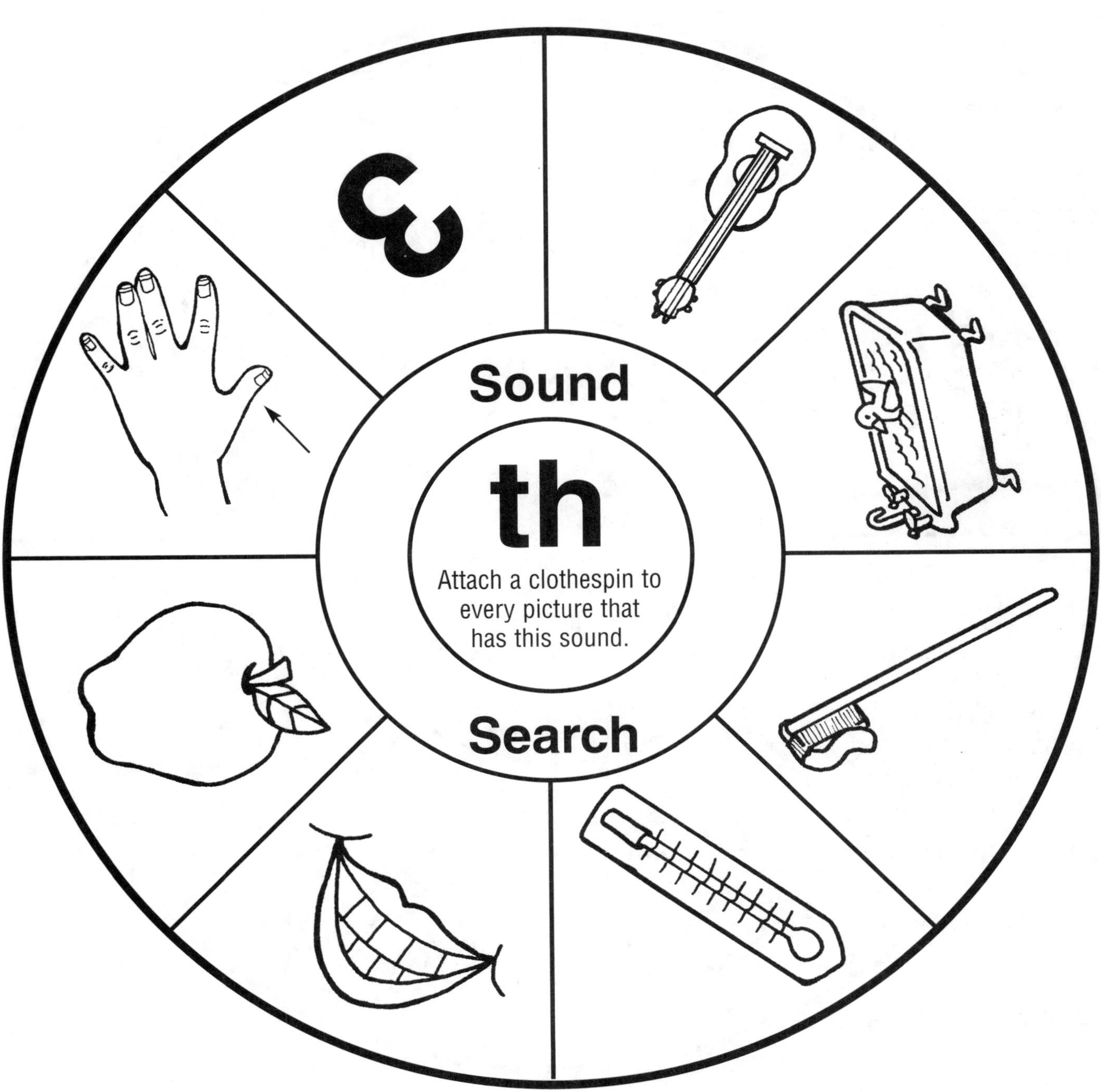

Sound Search (cont.)

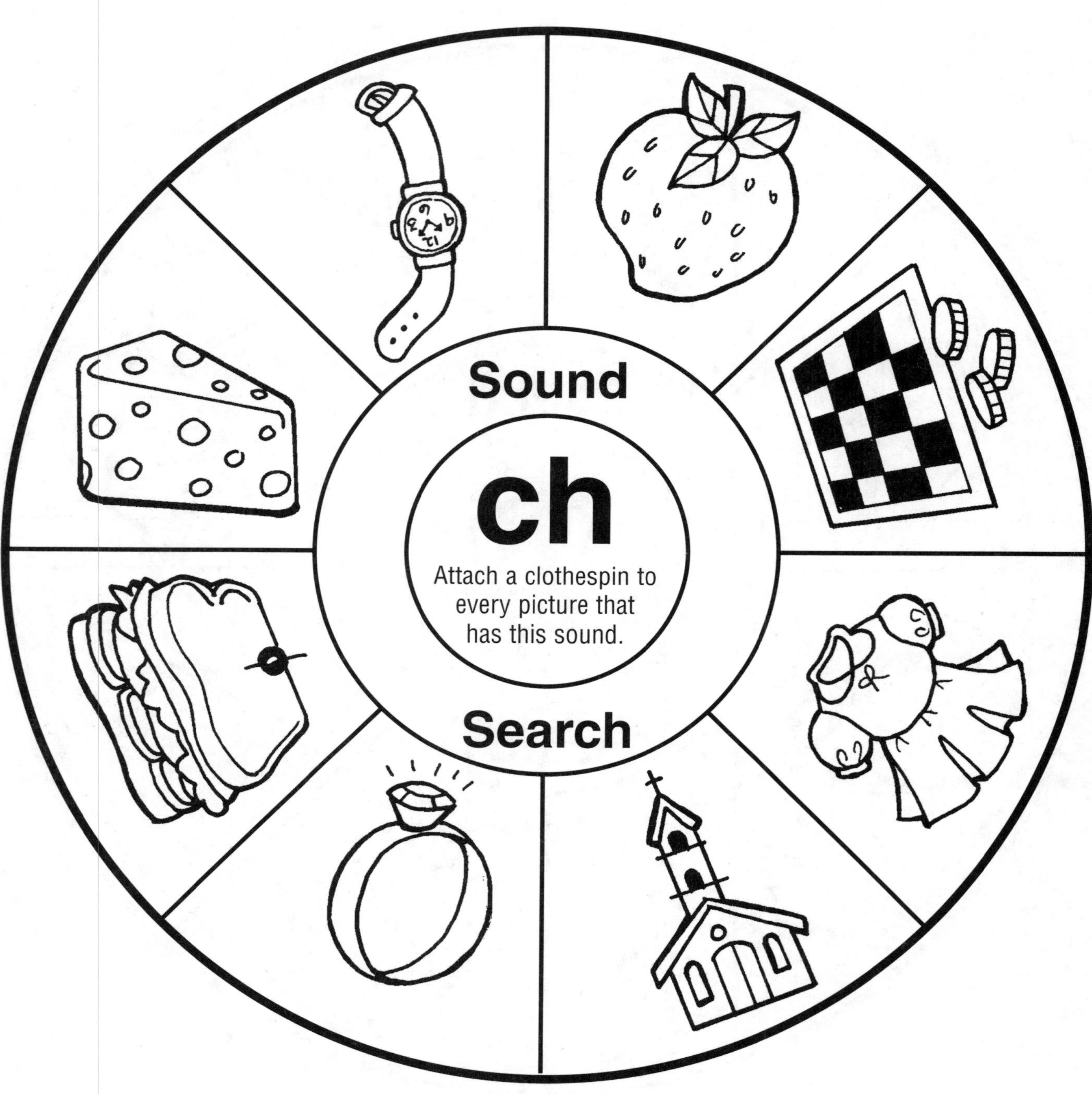

Sound Search (cont.)

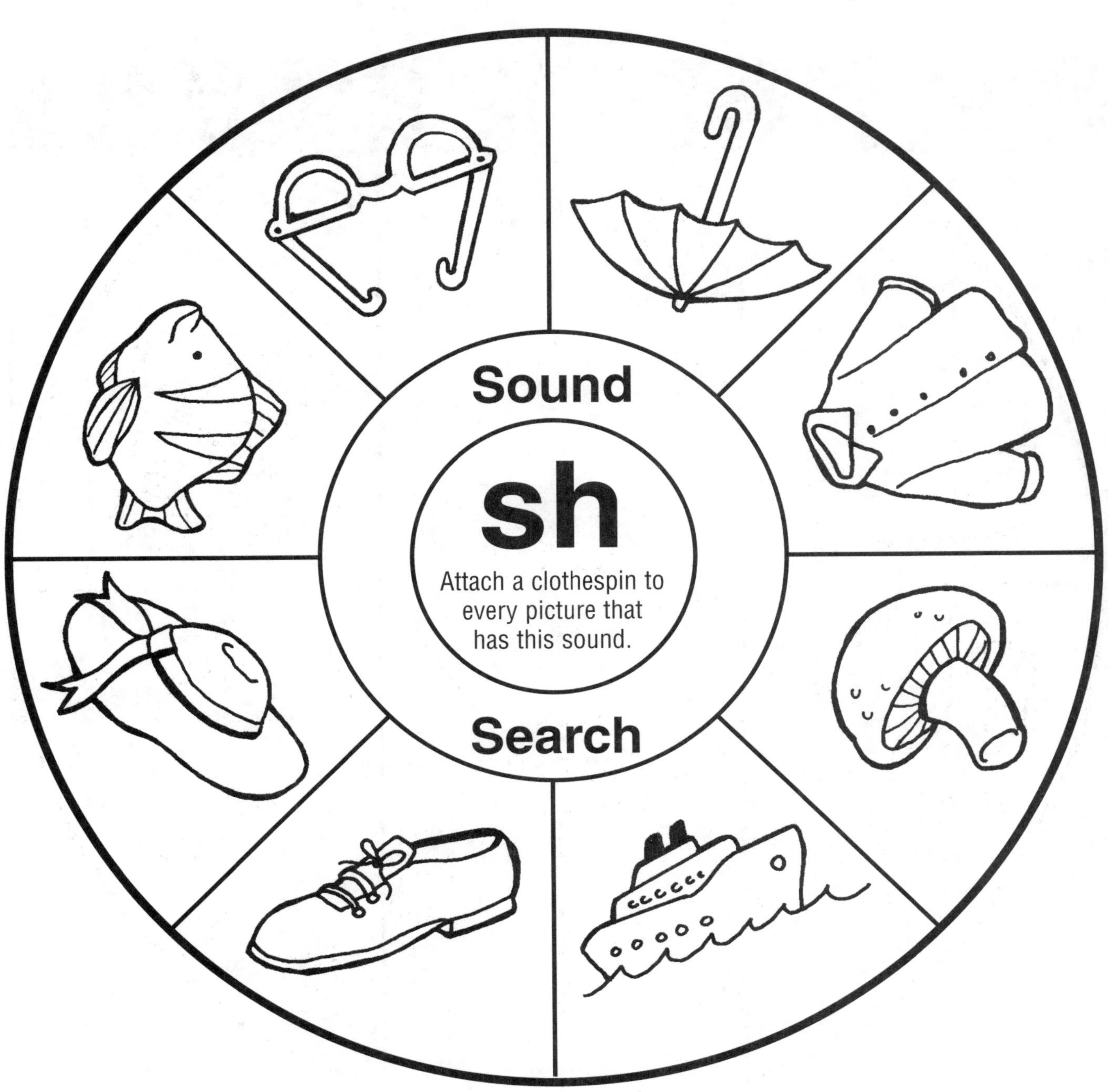

Sound Search (cont.)

Answer Sheet

Directions: For each sound, write the names of the pictures to which you attached the clothespins. Draw a picture to go with each word.

th	ch	sh

Wheel of Words

Skills: blending short vowel words

blending words that begin with digraphs or blends

Materials

- copies of pages 50–56
- brads
- scissors
- pencils

Preparation

1. Choose one wheel (Short Vowels—pages 50 and 51, Blends and Digraphs—pages 52 and 53, or Make Your Own!—pages 54 and 55) to focus on during this lesson. Copy one Wheel of Words for each student.
2. Copy one answer sheet (page 56) for each student.

Procedure

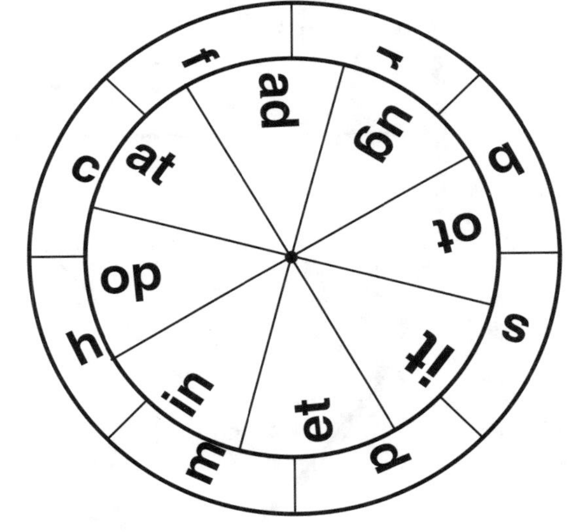

1. Ask the students to cut out both parts of their wheels. To assemble the wheels, help them place each smaller circle on top of a larger circle and then attach a brad to the center. The brads should be loose enough to allow the wheels to turn easily.
2. Show the students how to turn the center wheel to make words.
3. The students should write all of the combinations that they make on their answer sheets. They can then circle the words that are real words and cross off the words that are not real.
4. Tell the students to turn their wheels again and repeat the process.

(**Note:** For the wheel on pages 54 and 55, you might wish to choose theme words, sight words, spelling words, words with prefixes or suffixes, compound words, etc. Have students write their real-word combinations on a piece of paper.)

Writing Connections

- ✐ Ask each student to choose four or more words from the answer sheets and write them in a sentence. Have students illustrate their sentences.
- ✐ Challenge each student to use four or more words from the wheels in the dialogue bubbles of a comic strip.

Wheel of Words (cont.)

Short Vowels

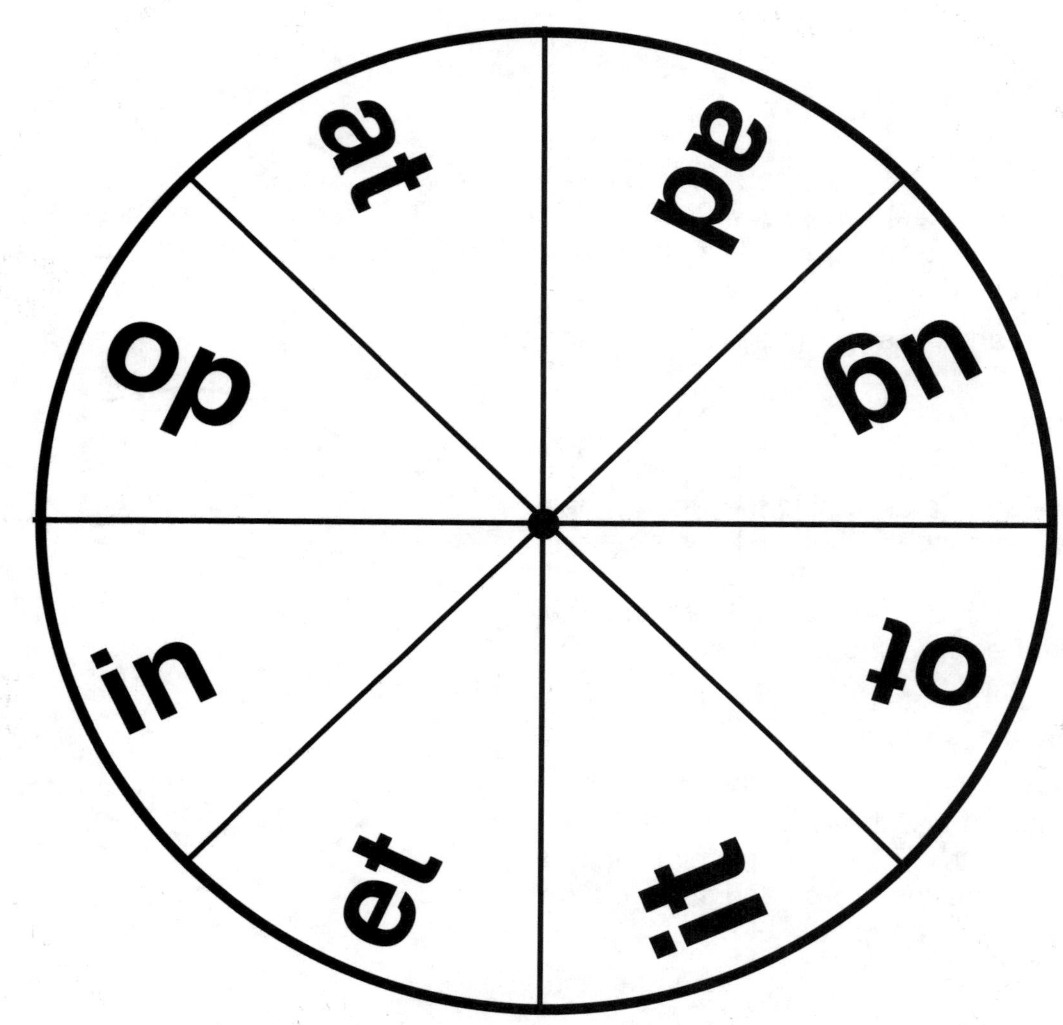

Wheel of Words (cont.)

Short Vowels

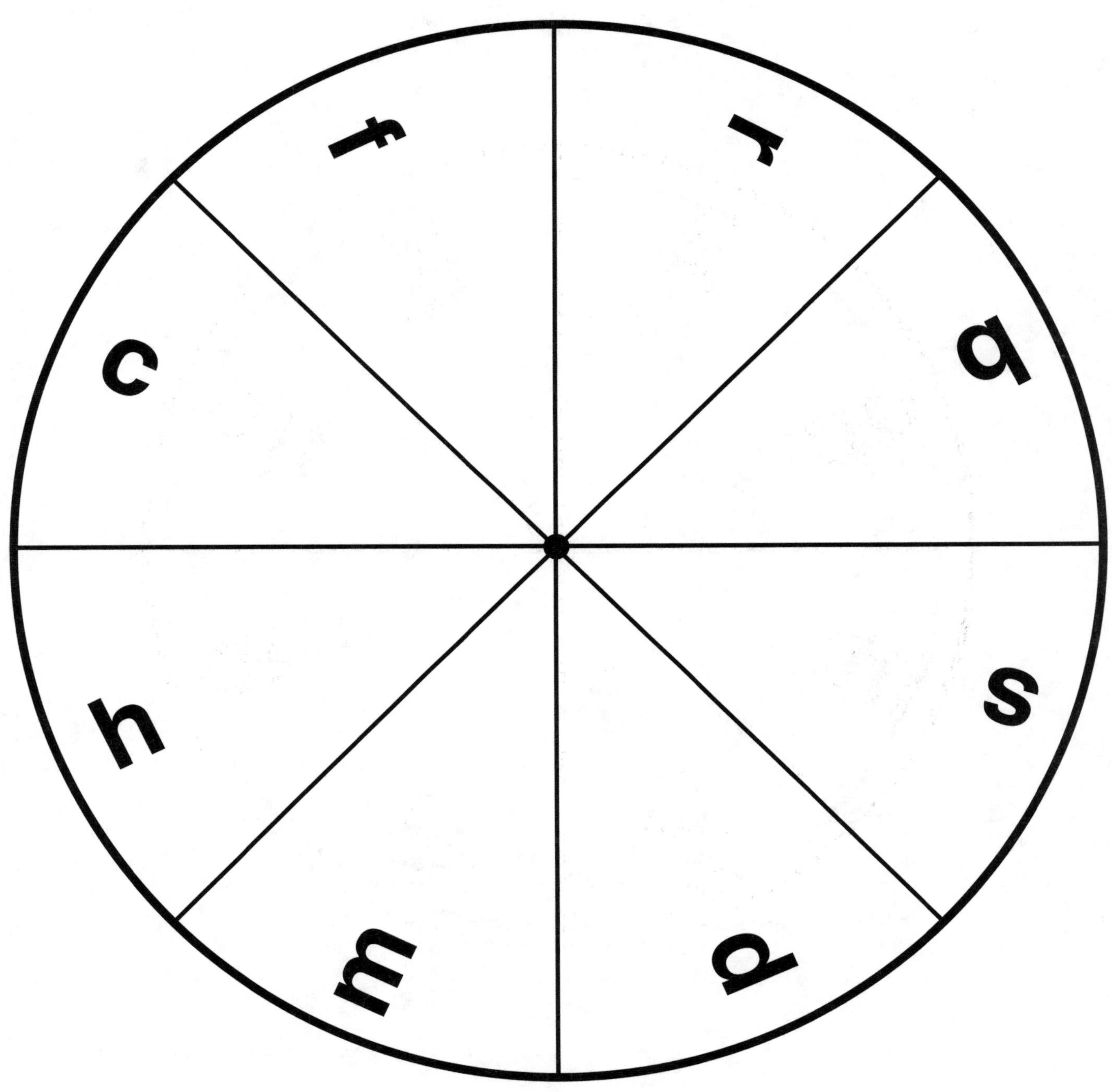

Wheel of Words (cont.)

Blends and Digraphs

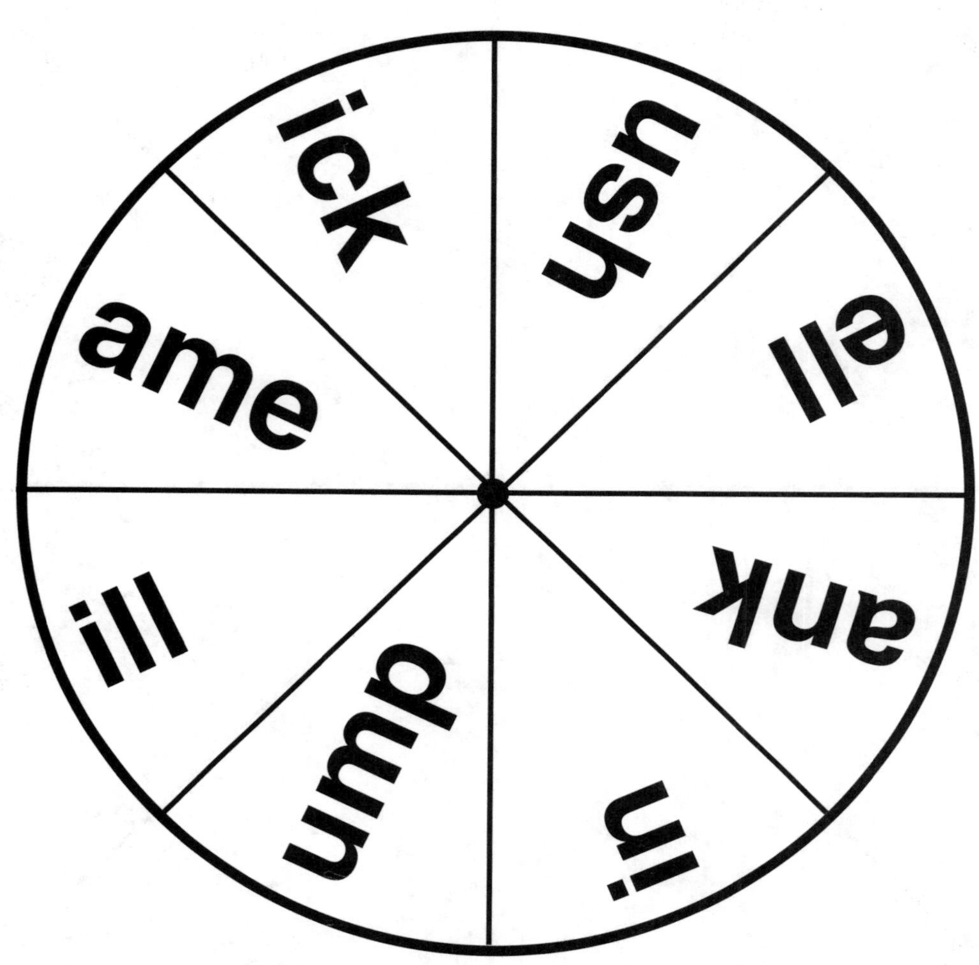

Wheel of Words (cont.)

Blends and Digraphs

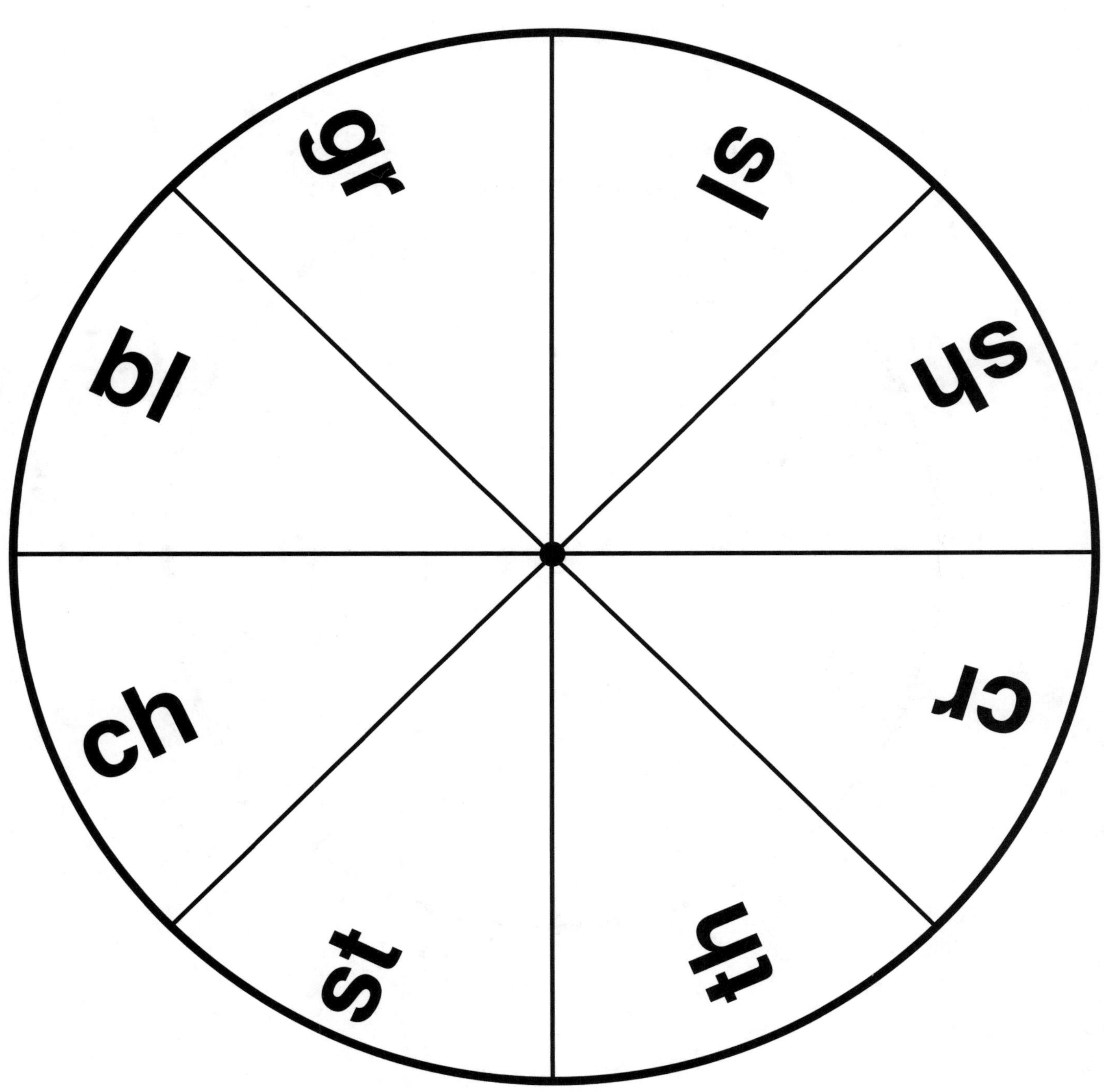

Wheel of Words (cont.)

Make Your Own!

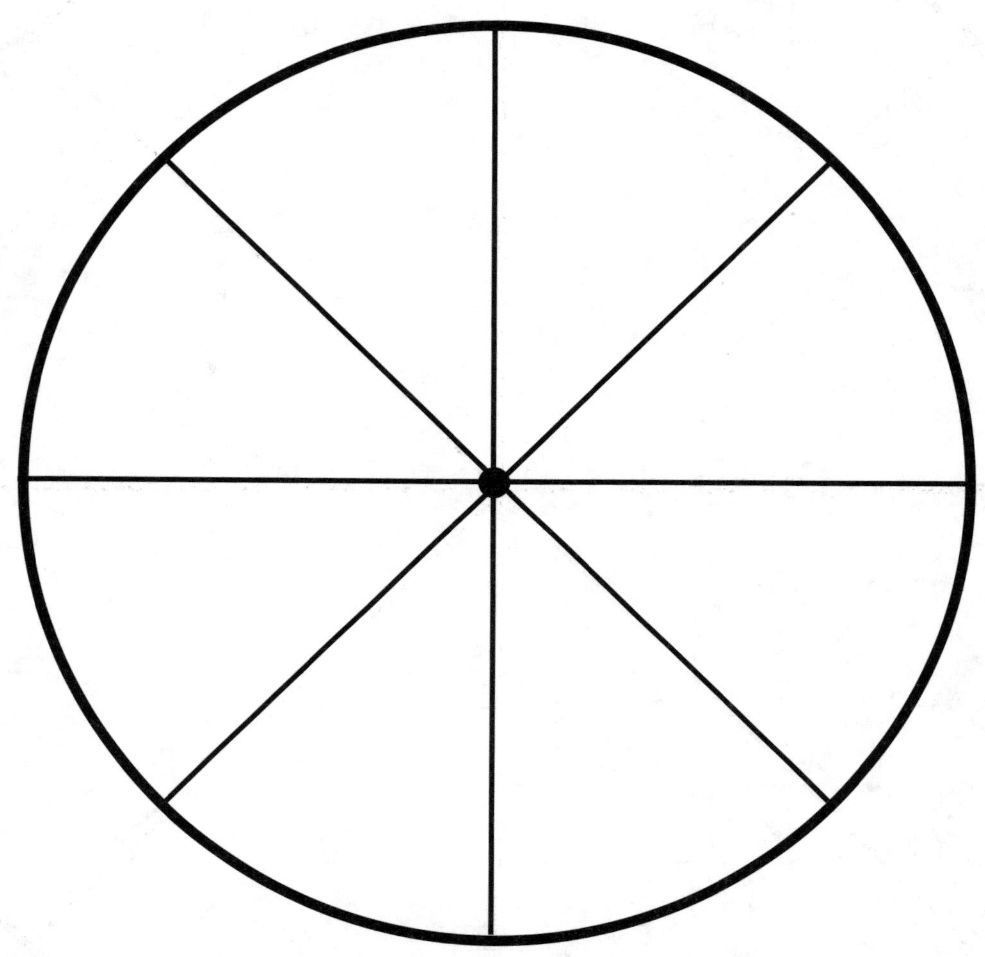

Wheel of Words (cont.)

Make Your Own!

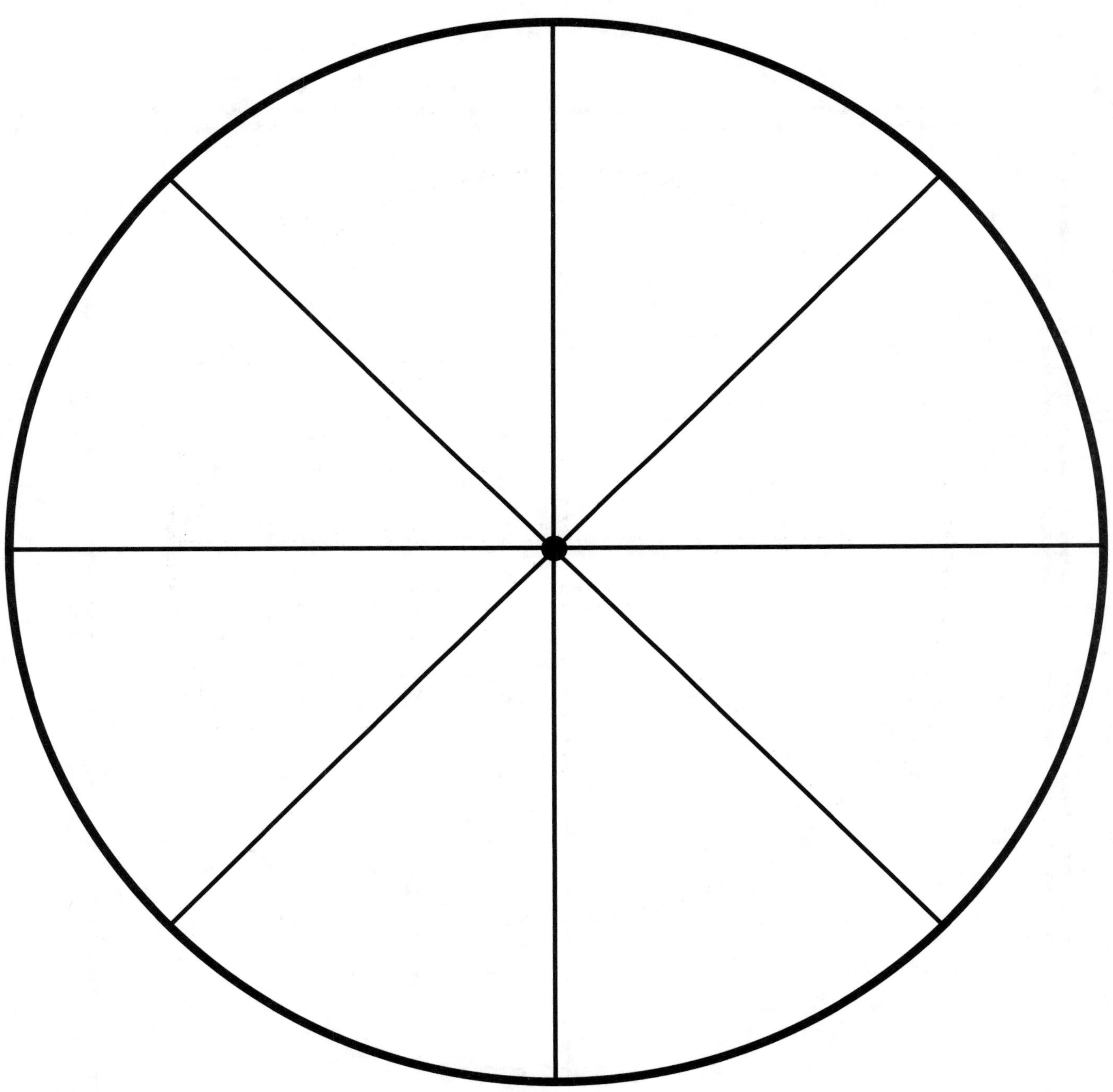

Wheel of Words (cont.)

Answer Sheet

Directions: Write down all of the letter combinations that you made on your word wheel. Circle the real words and cross out the words that are not real. Turn your wheel again and repeat the process.

Short Vowels	Blends and Digraphs
1. ______________	1. ______________
2. ______________	2. ______________
3. ______________	3. ______________
4. ______________	4. ______________
5. ______________	5. ______________
6. ______________	6. ______________
7. ______________	7. ______________
8. ______________	8. ______________

Word Race

Skill: repetition of spelling or sight words

Materials

- copies of pages 58–60
- poster board
- overhead transparency markers
- dice
- small items such as beans or buttons, to be used as game pieces (one per student)
- list of spelling or sight words
- crayons or markers (optional)

Preparation

1. Copy one set of pages 58–60 for each pair or group.
2. To assemble each game board, cut along the dashed line on page 59 and then tape it (on the back) to page 60.
3. Mount the game boards on heavy poster board. You may wish to add some color to the game boards with crayons or markers at this point, although it is not necessary.
4. Laminate the game boards.
5. Using an overhead transparency marker, write the desired words (you may wish to use a list of spelling or sight words that your class is currently studying) on each empty square. The words can then be erased at any time and new words added.

Procedure *(2–4 players)*

1. Review the word list that is the focus of your game.
2. Hand out all of the game materials to each pair or group.
3. Read and discuss the rules and directions (page 58) with the students.
4. Allow each pair or group a couple of practice plays before beginning the game.
5. Answer any questions.
6. Begin playing the game.

Variations

1. Write a digraph or blend in each board space. When a student lands on a space, his or her challenge will be to say and spell a word that has that digraph or blend sound. Keep a dictionary nearby for the students to check each other's answers.
2. This same game board can later be reused for practicing math facts. Instead of words, write equations in each box for the players to answer.

Word Race (cont.)

Object of the Game

The first person to get from his or her Home box, all the way around the board and back to Home is the winner.

How to Play Word Race

1. There are four Home boxes on the board. Each player chooses a different "Home" to start from by placing a game piece in that box.

2. Players roll the dice to see who goes first. The player with the highest number begins the game.

3. Each player, in turn, rolls the dice and moves (clockwise) the number of spaces indicated.

4. When a player lands on a space, he or she must read the word in the space out loud. If a player does not read the word correctly (as decided by the other players), he or she must move back to where the turn began.

5. If a second player lands on an already occupied space, the first player on the space gets bumped all the way back to his or her Home space.

6. If a player lands on a space which sends him or her to the hangar, that player must go to the hangar and wait for his or her next turn. If the player then rolls a 1, 3, or 5 on the next turn, he or she may return to the former space. Otherwise, the player must wait for another turn and try again until an odd number is rolled.

7. After going all the way around the board and back to his or her original starting space, a player must roll the exact number on the dice to get back into his or her "Home" space. The first person to do this is the winner.

Word Race (cont.)

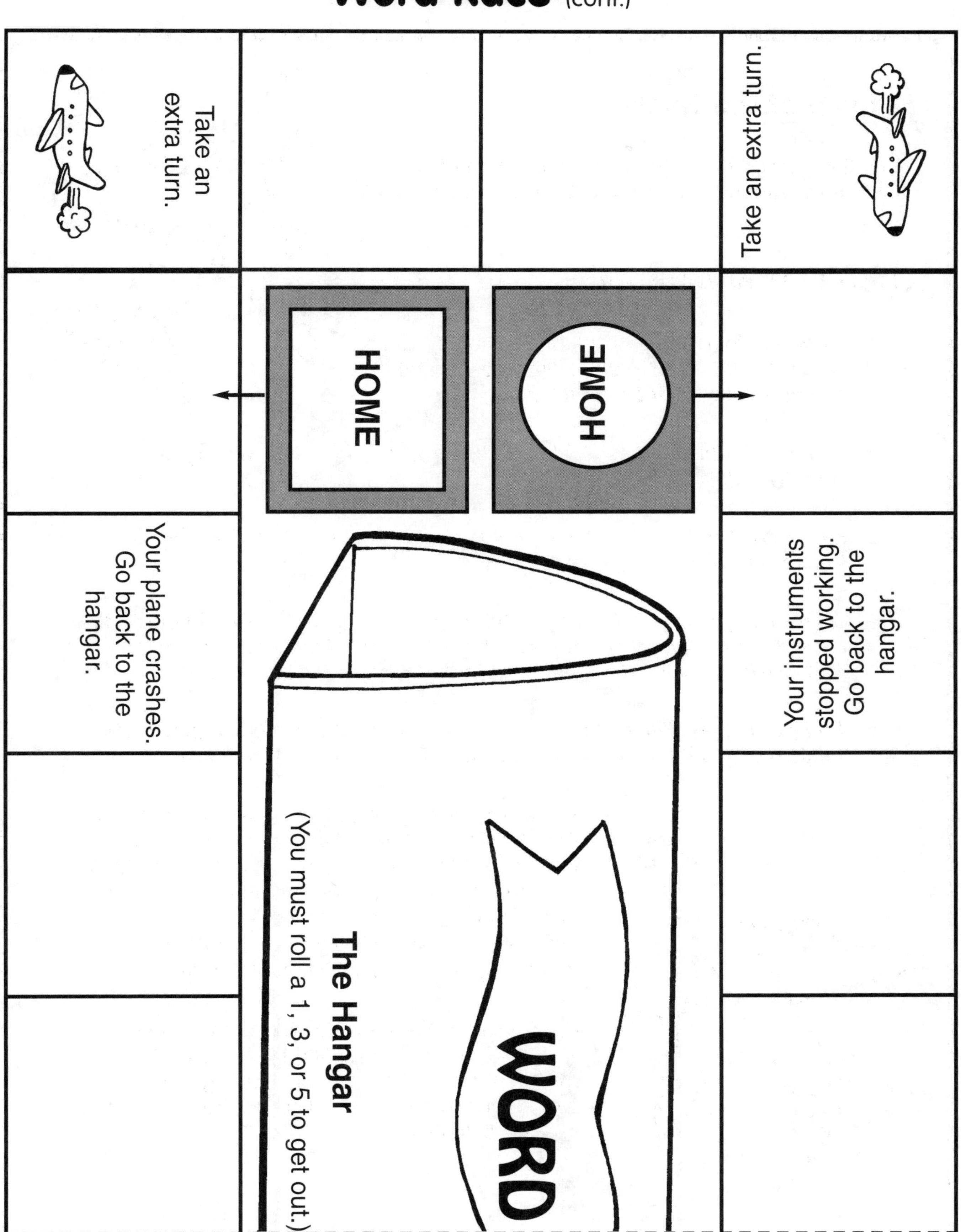

Cut along the dashed line.

Word Race (cont.)

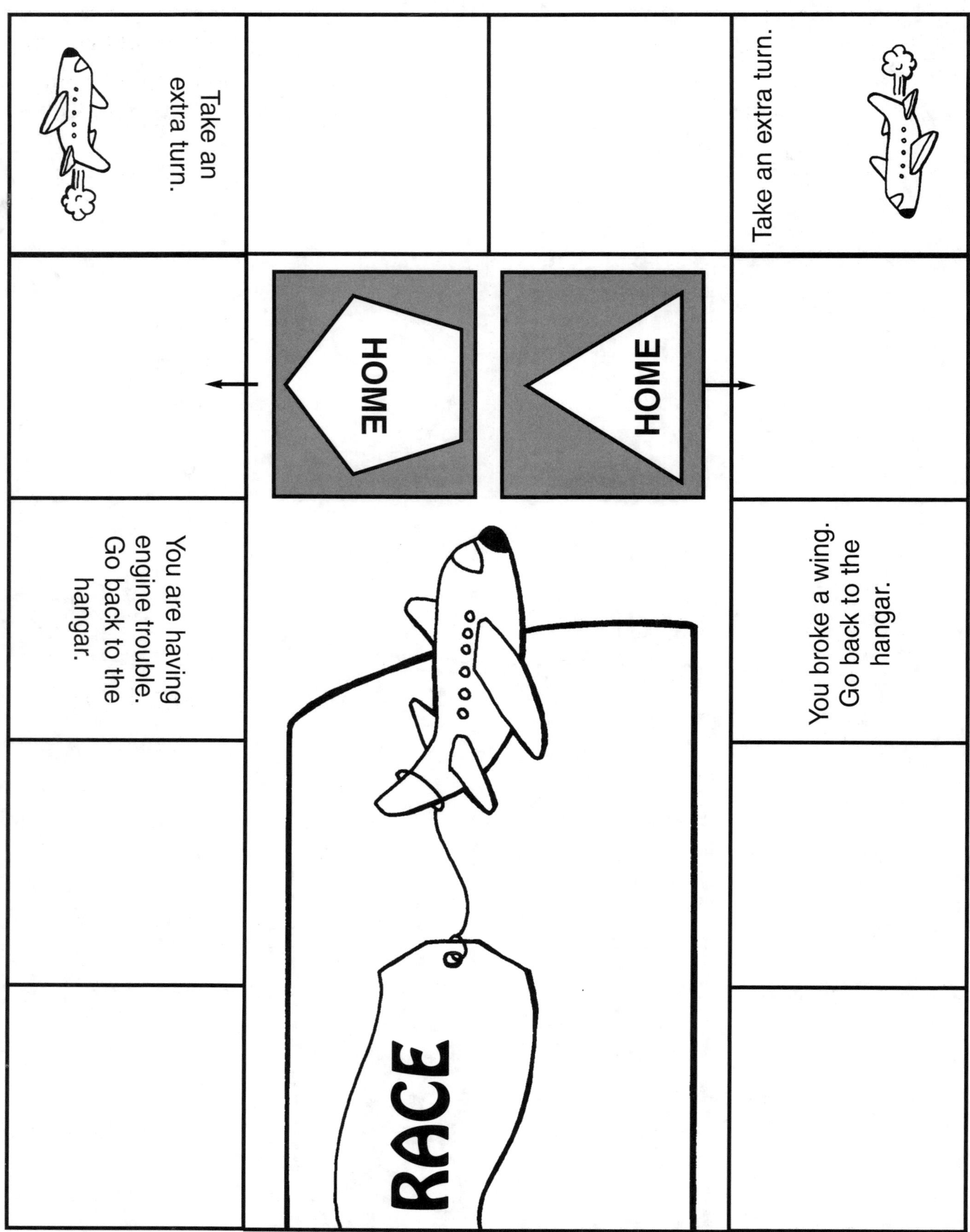

Tape the dashed line on page 59 to this line.

Roll-a-Word

Skills: blending short-vowel words

blending words that begin with a digraph or blend

Materials

- copies of pages 62–73 (Page 72 is optional.)
- heavy cardstock (red and green)
- tape
- scissors
- pencils

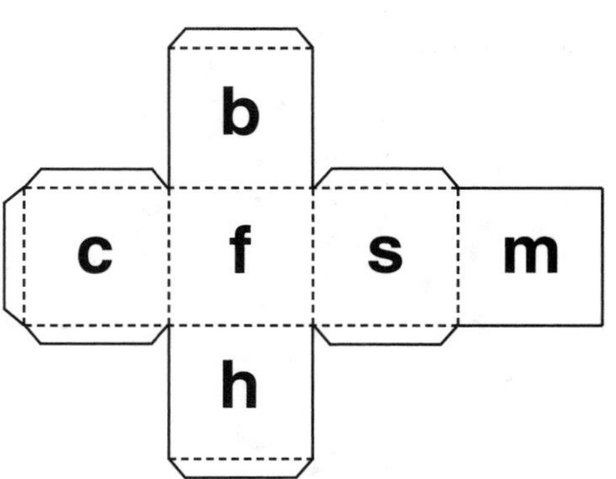

Preparation

1. Copy the desired Roll-a-Word dice outlines onto cardstock. You may wish to copy the word beginnings on green (go) and the word endings pages on red (stop). If you would rather create your own dice using theme words, sight words, spelling words, words with prefixes or suffixes, compound words, etc., use the outline on page 72.
2. Copy one answer sheet (page 73) for each student.
3. Cut out the dice. Laminate them if you wish to use them again in the future. Assemble the dice using tape.

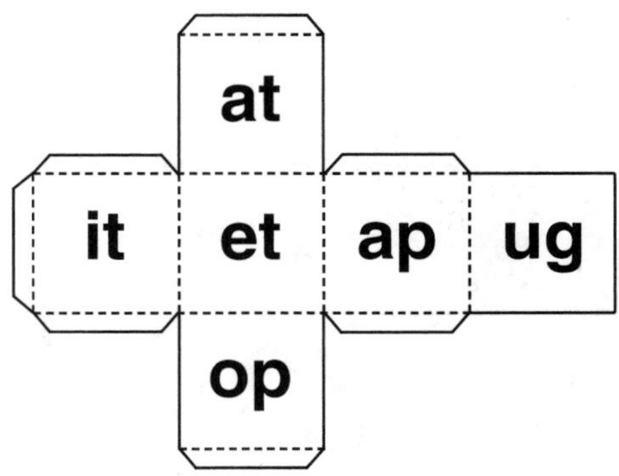

Procedure

1. The students roll one red (word endings) and one green (word beginnings) block and then blend the beginning and ending sounds together to make a word.
2. Next, the students write on their answer sheets (page 73) each word that they make. When they are through, ask them to circle the words that are real and cross off the words that are not.

Writing Connections

- Ask each student to use three or four of the dice words in a story. Encourage students to also illustrate their stories.
- Challenge each student to use three or four of the dice words in a single sentence. These sentences may then be illustrated.

Roll-a-Word (cont.)

Short Vowels—Beginnings

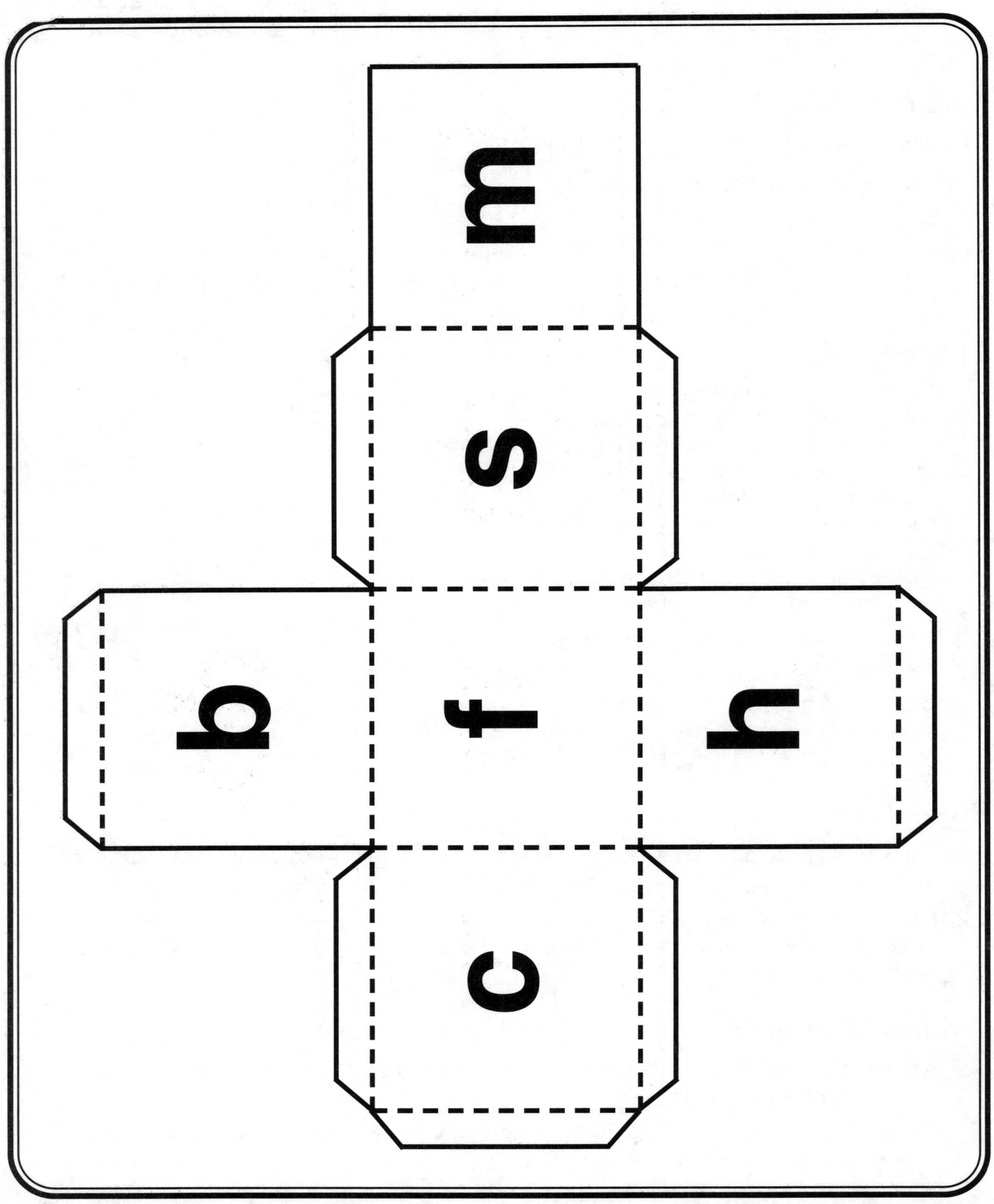

Roll-a-Word (cont.)

Short Vowels—Endings

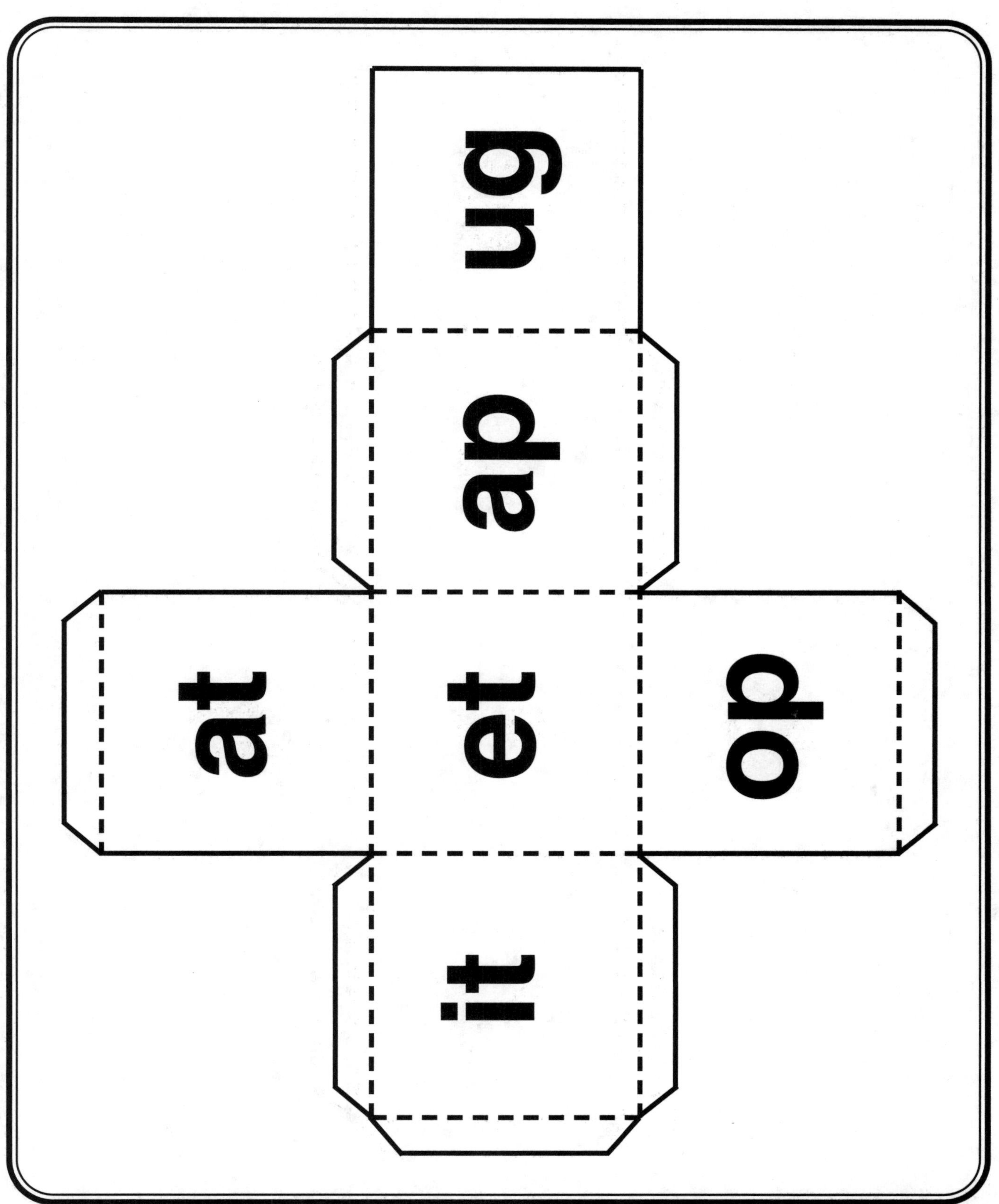

Roll-a-Word (cont.)

Digraphs—Beginnings

Roll-a-Word (cont.)

Digraphs—Endings

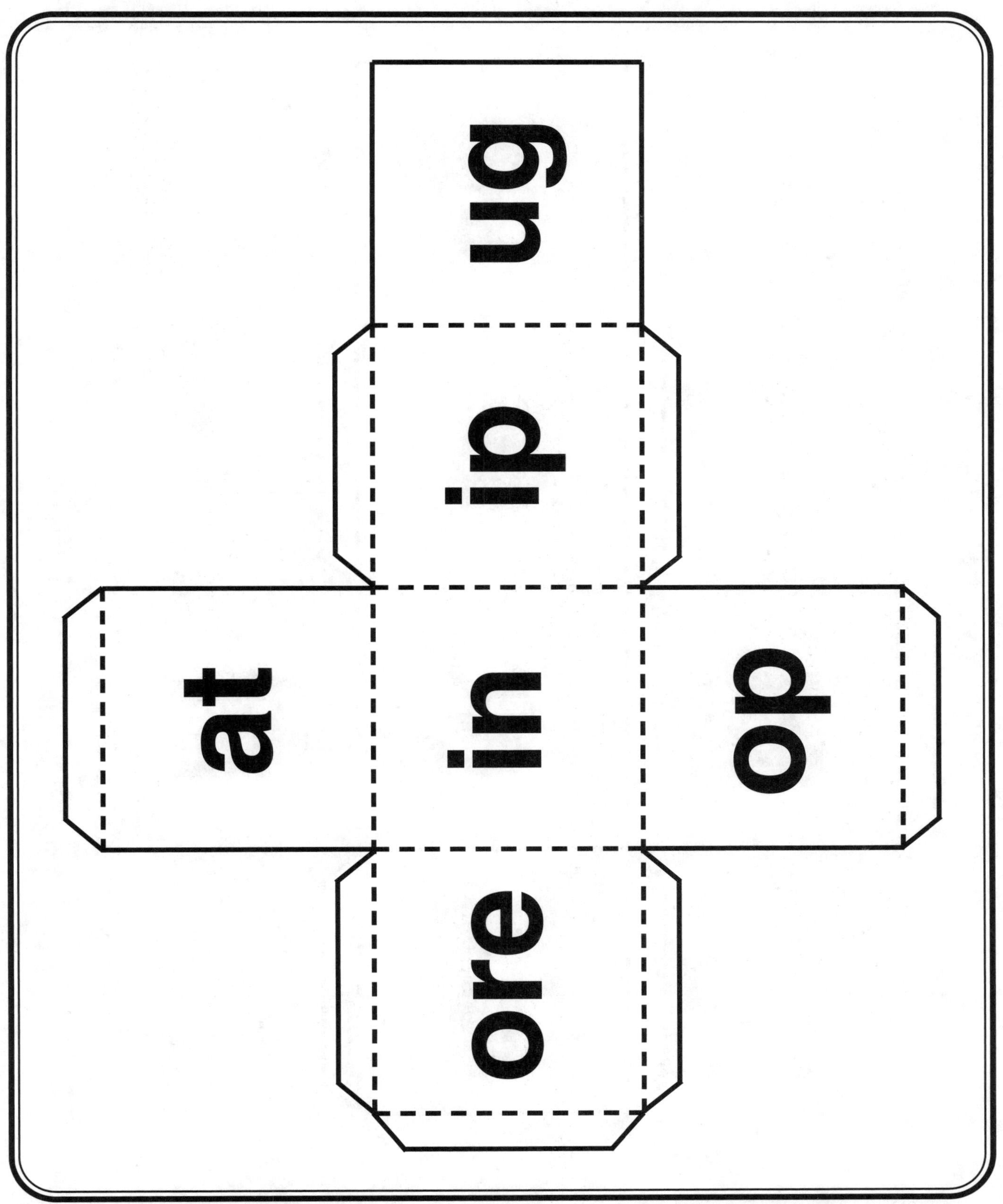

Roll-a-Word (cont.)

Blends: Level One—Beginnings

Roll-a-Word (cont.)

Blends: Level One—Endings

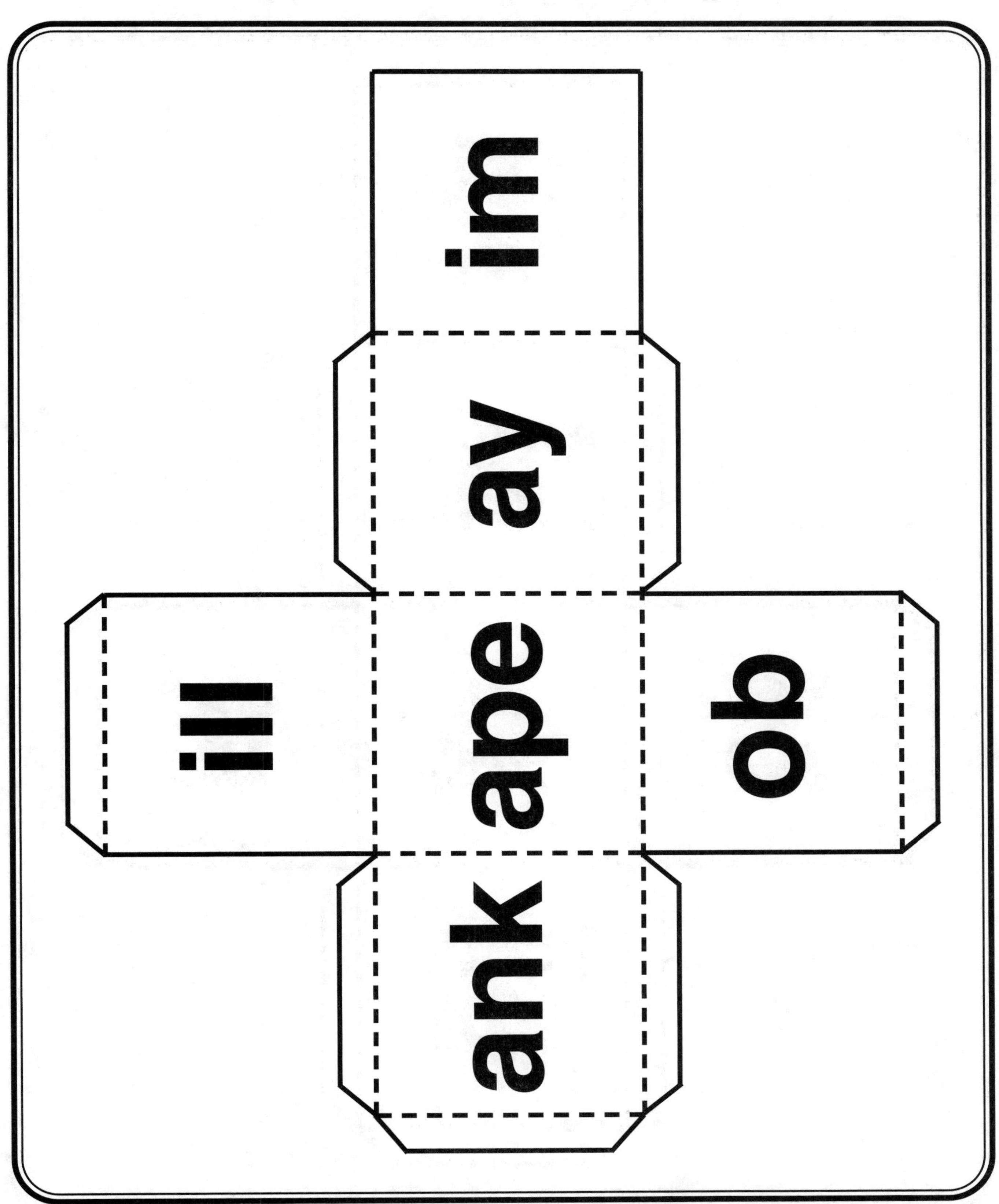

Roll-a-Word (cont.)

Blends: Level Two—Beginnings

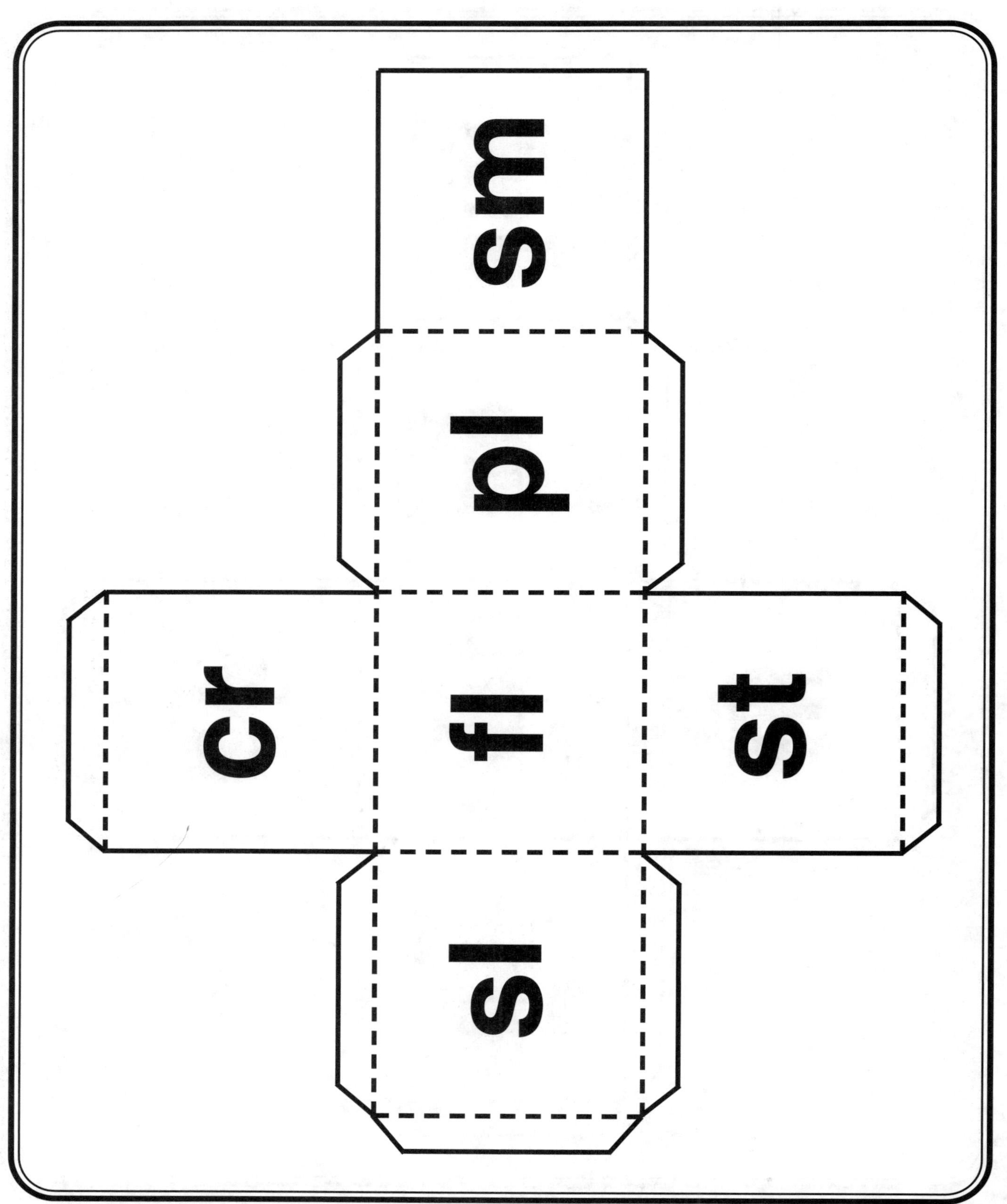

Roll-a-Word (cont.)

Blends: Level Two—Endings

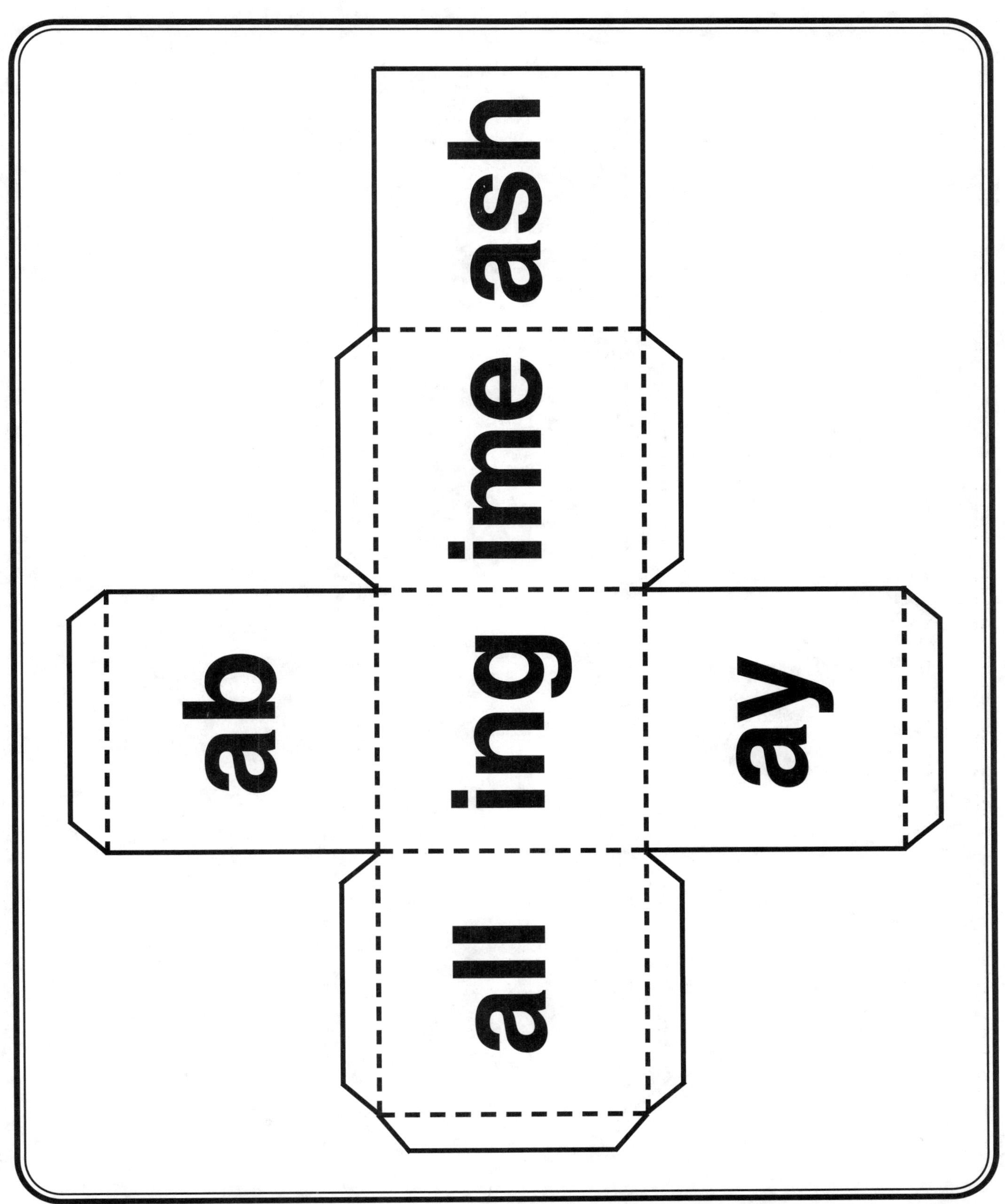

Roll-a-Word (cont.)

Blends: Level Three—Beginnings

Roll-a-Word (cont.)

Blends: Level Three—Endings

Roll-a-Word (cont.)

Make Your Own!

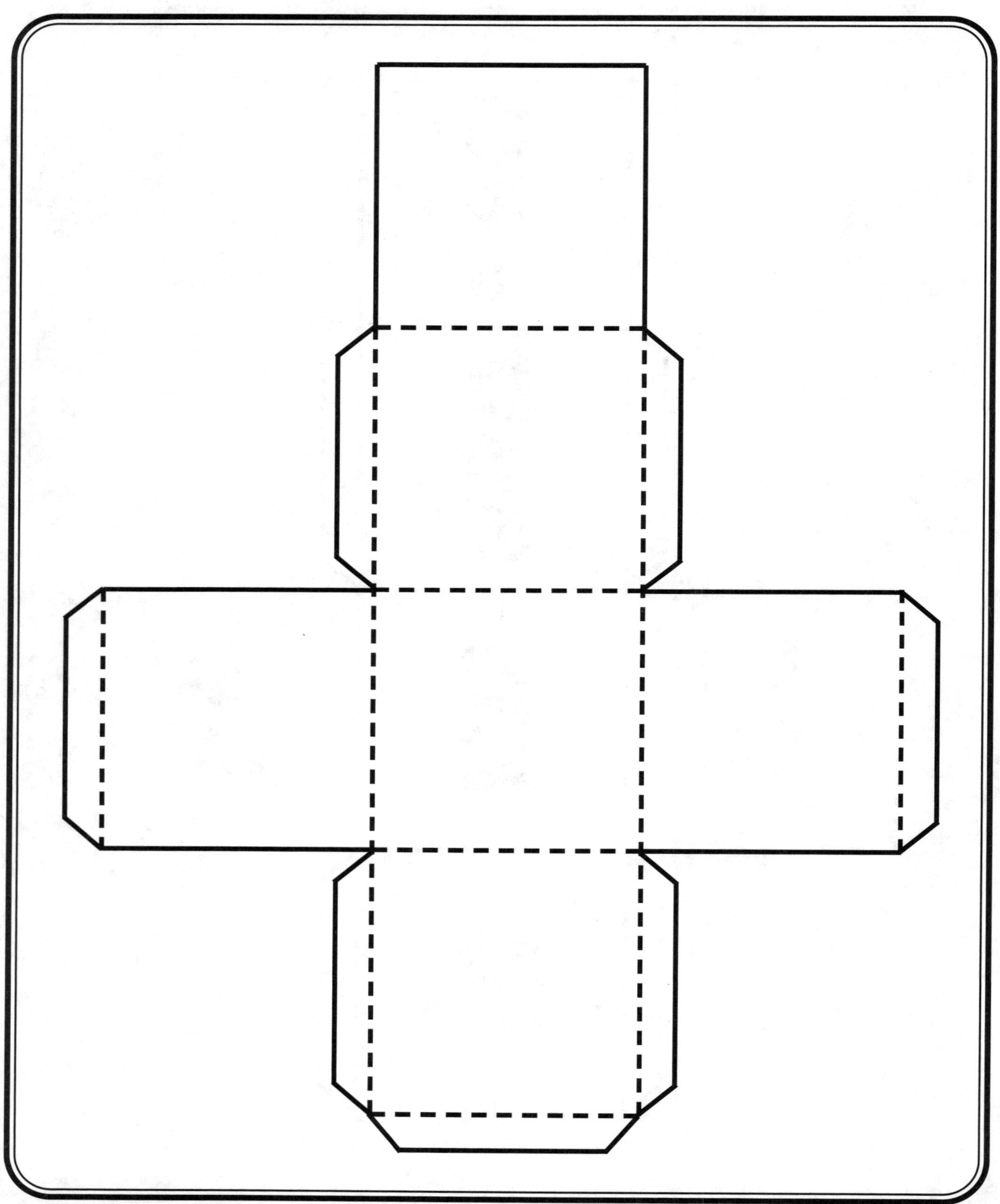

Roll-a-Word (cont.)

Answer Sheet

Directions: Write down each of the words that you roll. Circle the words that are real and cross out the ones that are not real.

1. ____________________
2. ____________________
3. ____________________
4. ____________________
5. ____________________
6. ____________________
7. ____________________
8. ____________________
9. ____________________
10. ____________________
11. ____________________
12. ____________________
13. ____________________
14. ____________________
15. ____________________
16. ____________________

Vowel Search

Skill: discrimination of short and long vowel sounds

Materials

- copies of pages 75–88
- scissors
- pencils
- pocket chart (optional for group use)

Preparation

1. Copy pages 75–84 on heavy cardstock. Make one set for every group or center.
2. Cut out the cards and laminate them so that they last longer.
3. Copy the activity sheet(s) of your choice (pages 85–88). Make one copy for each student.

Procedure

1. Tell the students to place the picture cards under the appropriate vowel cards. For example, the picture card of a fox would go under short vowels and then under the short "o" card. (You may want to use one or two vowels at a time for this activity. Later, use all the vowels for a review.)
2. Ask the students to write the picture card names under the appropriate vowels on the activity sheets.

Writing Connections

- Ask the students to each write a poem using four or more words from the activity sheet(s). They may then illustrate their poems.
- Tell the students to find a partner. Ask each pair to write a script for a television commercial. The commercials must include four words from their activity sheets. Have them perform their commercials for the class.

Vowel Search (cont.)

Long Vowels

Short Vowels

o **as in pot** 	**o** **as in rope**
u **as in cup** 	**u** **as in tube** 

Vowel Search (cont.)

e

as in net

a

as in rain

e

as in bee 

i

as in fish

a

as in apple

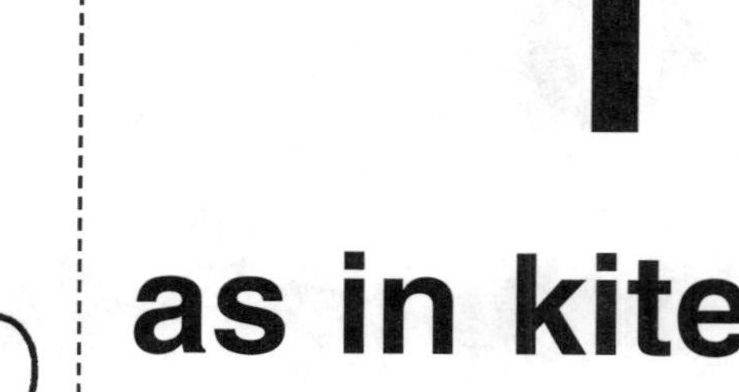

i

as in kite 

Vowel Search (cont.)

Vowel Search (cont.)

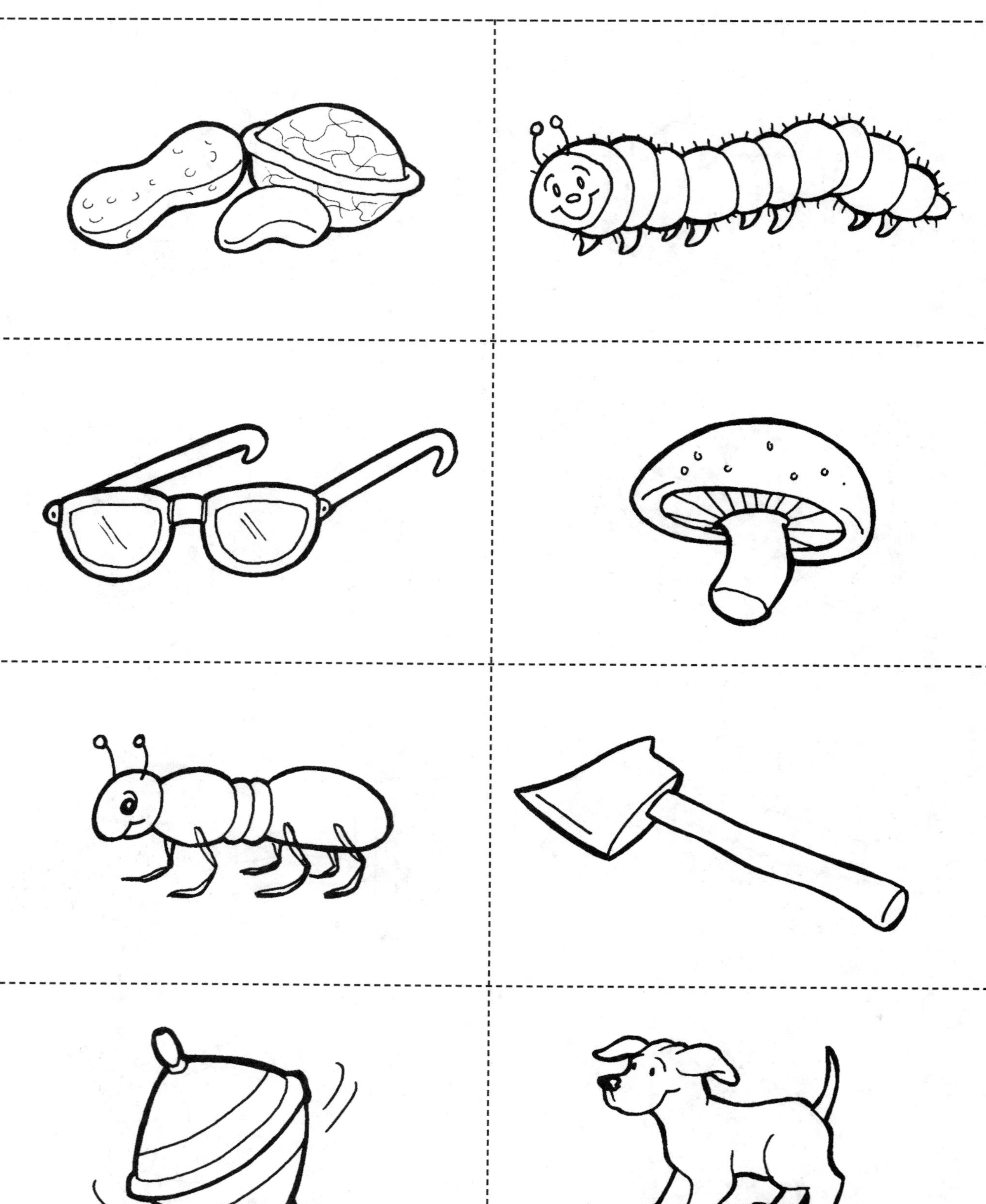

Vowel Search (cont.)

Vowel Search (cont.)

Vowel Search (cont.)

Vowel Search (cont.)

Vowel Search (cont.)

Vowel Search (cont.)

Vowel Search (cont.)

Directions: Write the names of the picture cards underneath their vowel sounds.

ă as in apple	ā as in rain	ŏ as in pot

Vowel Search (cont.)

Directions: Write the names of the picture cards underneath their vowel sounds.

ō as in rope	ĭ as in fish	ī as in kite

Vowel Search (cont.)

Directions: Write the names of the picture cards underneath their vowel sounds.

ŭ as in cup	ū as in tube	ĕ as in net	ē as in bee

Vowel Search (cont.)

Short and Long Vowels

Directions: Write the names of the picture cards underneath their vowel sounds.

Short Vowels	Long Vowels

Compound Fun

Skill: compound identification

Materials

- copies of pages 90–100
- pencils
- scissors
- pocket chart (optional for group use)

Preparation

1. Decide if this activity will be a center activity, an individual activity, or a whole group activity. Copy one set of pages 90–99 for each student or center or just a single set if you are working with the class as a whole. Make the copies on cardstock or any other type of heavy paper.
2. Cut out the strips and cards from the copies. If you wish, laminate them for durability.
3. Make a copy of page 100 for each student.

Procedure

1. Ask the students to study the compound picture equations. Tell them to search for the word and picture cards that go with the equations. For example:

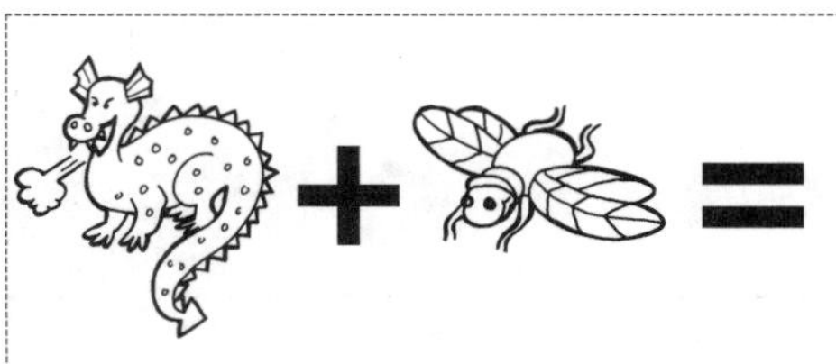

dragonfly

2. When they have decoded the equations, give each student a copy of page 100. On this activity sheet they will write the correct compound words and then draw pictures of the words.

Writing Connections

- Ask the students to each choose three or four compound words to use in a story. They may include illustrations with their stories.
- Challenge the students to write their own songs, using three or four compound words from this activity. Allow them to perform their songs for the class if they desire.

Compound Fun (cont.)

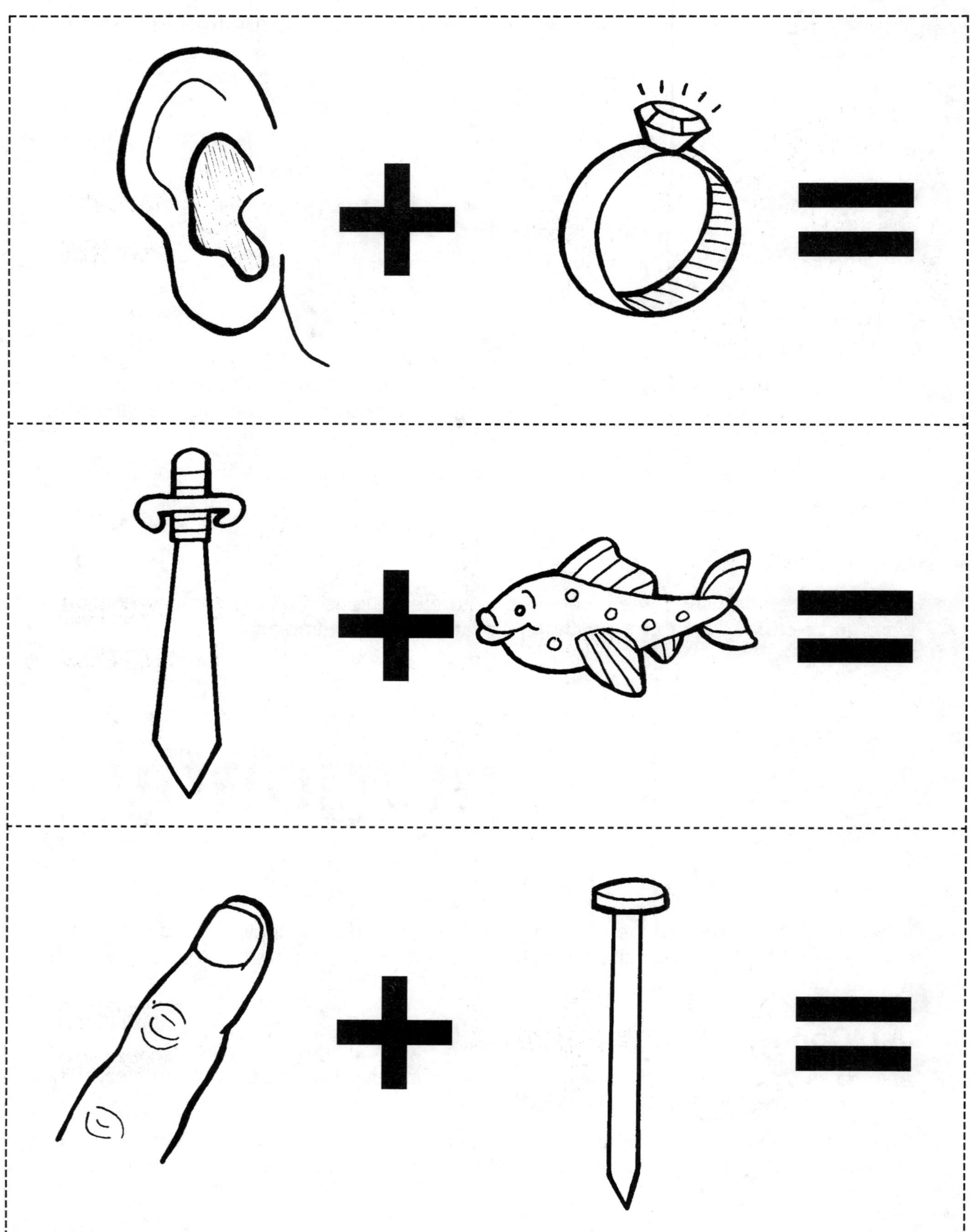

Compound Fun (cont.)

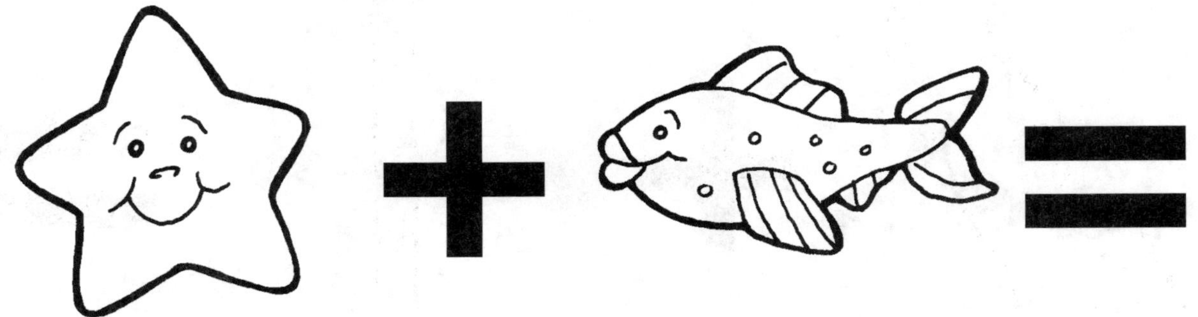

Compound Fun (cont.)

Compound Fun (cont.)

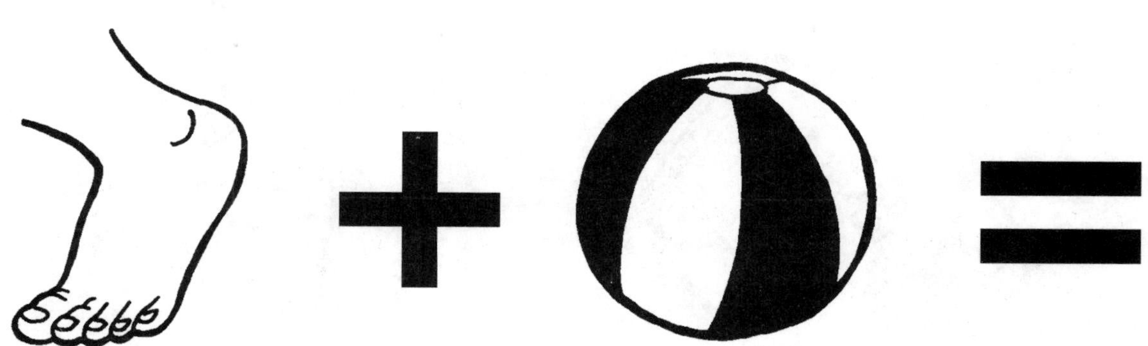

Compound Fun (cont.)

Compound Fun (cont.)

Compound Fun (cont.)

snowman

swordfish

cowboy

Compound Fun (cont.)

cupcake	football	starfish

Compound Fun (cont.)

fingernail

dragonfly

ladybug

Compound Fun (cont.)

rainbow	fireman	earring

Compound Fun (cont.)

Directions: Solve the compound word equations. Write the answers on the lines below and then draw pictures of the words in the boxes.

Example: ladybug 

1. ________

2. ________

3. ________

4. ________

5. ________

6. ________

7. ________

8. ________

9. ________

10. ________

11. ________

12. ________

Phonics Game

Vowel Fish

Skill: vowel discrimination

Materials

- a set of Picture Vowel Fish cards (pages 102–109) or Vowel Fish (pages 110–119) for every two students
- scissors
- crayons (optional)

Preparation

1. Copy the Vowel Fish or Picture Vowel Fish cards onto heavy paper. (**Note:** The cards, as ordered in this book, become progressively harder. Before you photocopy them, you may wish to review the cards to decide just how difficult you want the game to be.)
2. Color the pictures, if you desire. Cut out the cards along the dashed lines. You may want to laminate them for durability.

Procedure *(2 players)*

Picture Vowel Fish

1. Each player gets five Picture Vowel Fish cards. The rest of the cards are placed, face down in the center of the table.
2. Player one asks player two, "Do you have a card that has the same sound the (*vowel on the picture card*) makes in the word (*name of the picture on the card*)?" Player two must then look through his or her cards and gives player one a card which has the same vowel sound. For example, player one might ask "Do you have a card that has the same sound that the 'u' makes in the word 'cup'?" Player two might give player one the card with the picture of nuts, which also has a short "u."
3. If player two does not have the card that was requested, he or she must say, "Go Vowel Fish." Player one must then draw from the pile of cards in the middle of the table. If the player draws a matching card, he or she gets an extra turn.
4. If a player gives another player the wrong card (for example, a word with a long "u" instead of a short "u"), he or she gets the card back.
5. The players continue taking turns until the pile of cards in the center of the table is gone. The winner is the person with the most sets of matching vowel cards.

Vowel Fish

1. Use the game rules described above. This game is more difficult. The players read the words and match the underlined vowels on the cards. For words with two or more vowel sounds, players must indicate the sound and letters represented in the word. For example, to find a match fo the word soap, the player might ask, "Do you have a card with the same sound that the 'oa' makes in soap?" There will be several word choices, such as rose, bone, potato, etc. If the other player has a matching word, he or she must identify the sound in the word and give up the matching card.
2. If a player "fishes" and finds a match, he or she must first indentify the matching sound before claiming the card.

Vowel Fish (cont.)

Picture Vowel Fish Cards

Vowel Fish (cont.)

Picture Vowel Fish Cards *(cont.)*

Vowel Fish (cont.)

Picture Vowel Fish Cards *(cont.)*

Vowel Fish (cont.)

Picture Vowel Fish Cards *(cont.)*

Vowel Fish (cont.)

Picture Vowel Fish Cards (cont.)

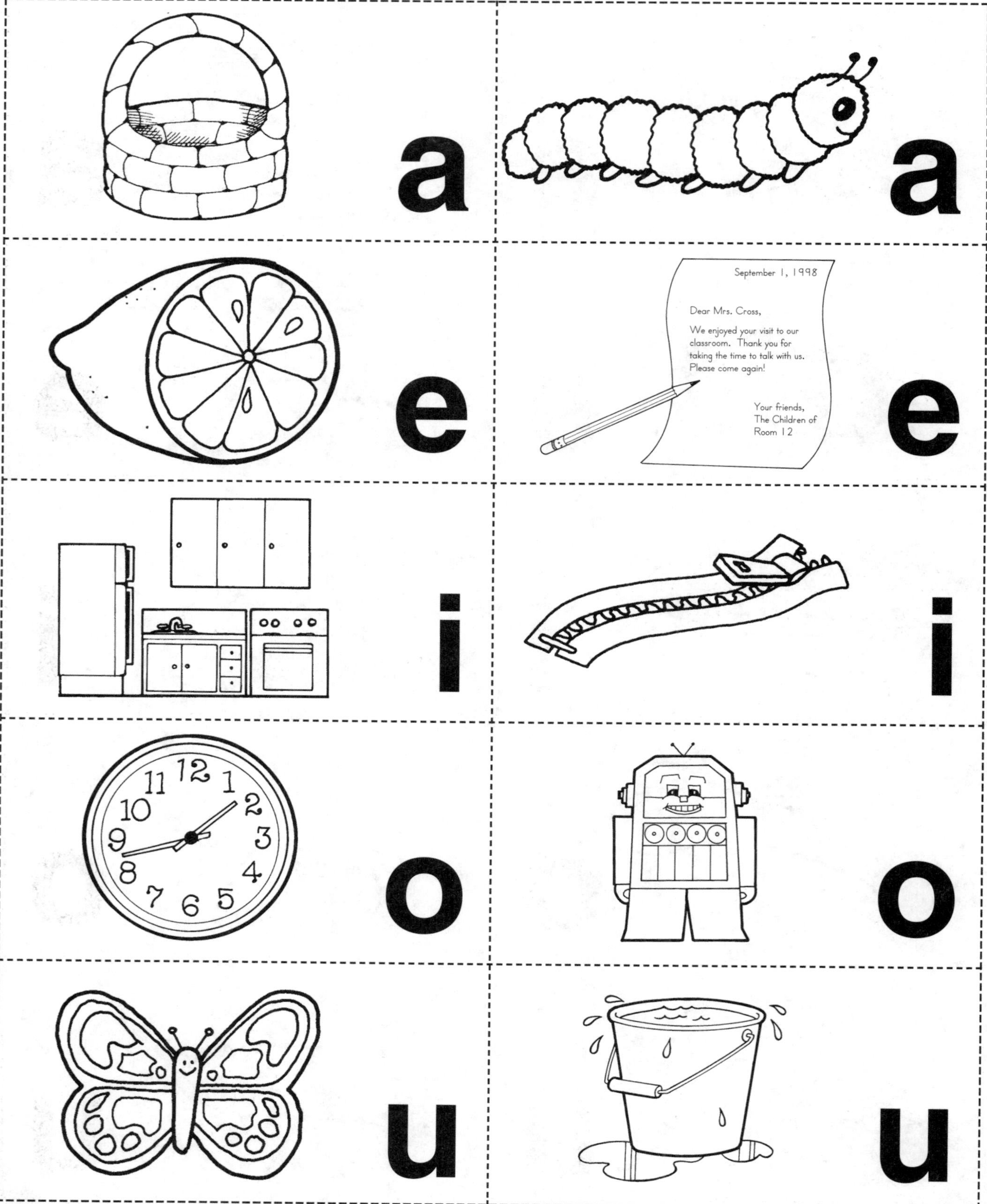

Vowel Fish (cont.)

Picture Vowel Fish Cards *(cont.)*

Vowel Fish (cont.)

Picture Vowel Fish Cards *(cont.)*

Vowel Fish (cont.)

Picture Vowel Fish Cards *(cont.)*

Vowel Fish (cont.)

Vowel Fish Cards

rat	ant
log	dot
rip	sit
tub	hut
set	pen

Vowel Fish (cont.)

Vowel Fish Cards *(cont.)*

hat	ax
mop	fox
pig	wig
cup	jug
net	bed

Vowel Fish (cont.)

Vowel Fish Cards *(cont.)*

cat	**man**
pot	**dog**
tin	**fit**
sun	**rug**
bet	**leg**

Vowel Fish (cont.)

Vowel Fish Cards *(cont.)*

acorn	cake
we	bee
bike	site
note	rope
huge	cube

Vowel Fish (cont.)

Vowel Fish Cards *(cont.)*

f<u>a</u>ce	<u>a</u>pron
k<u>e</u>y	s<u>ee</u>d
p<u>i</u>e	k<u>i</u>te
b<u>o</u>ne	n<u>o</u>se
c<u>u</u>te	t<u>u</u>be

Vowel Fish (cont.)

Vowel Fish Cards *(cont.)*

rake	game
leaf	seal
iron	fire
soap	snow
rose	yo-yo

Vowel Fish (cont.)

Vowel Fish Cards *(cont.)*

queen	**zebra**
unicorn	**flute**
spider	**tiger**
potato	**snowman**
grapes	**table**

Vowel Fish (cont.)

Vowel Fish Cards *(cont.)*

basket	glass
helmet	letter
bridge	zipper
clock	olive
button	truck

Vowel Fish (cont.)

Vowel Fish Cards *(cont.)*

hammer	dragon
lemon	pencil
quilt	twins
bottle	socks
bucket	umbrella

Vowel Fish (cont.)

Vowel Fish Cards *(cont.)*

sn<u>a</u>ke	pl<u>a</u>ne
l<u>ea</u>ves	tr<u>ee</u>
d<u>i</u>nosaur	f<u>i</u>reman
sp<u>o</u>kes	g<u>oa</u>t
tr<u>i</u>cycle	v<u>i</u>olin

Rhyme Wheels

Skills: blending rhymes
vocabulary expansion

Materials

- copies of pages 121–144
- brads/paper fasteners
- scissors
- crayons (optional)

Preparation

1. Choose which rhyming word wheel(s) you would like to focus on in this activity. Copy the desired wheel(s). Make one for each student or center.
2. Copy a set of the activity sheets from pages 143 and 144 for each student.
3. Laminate wheels for use in centers.

Procedure

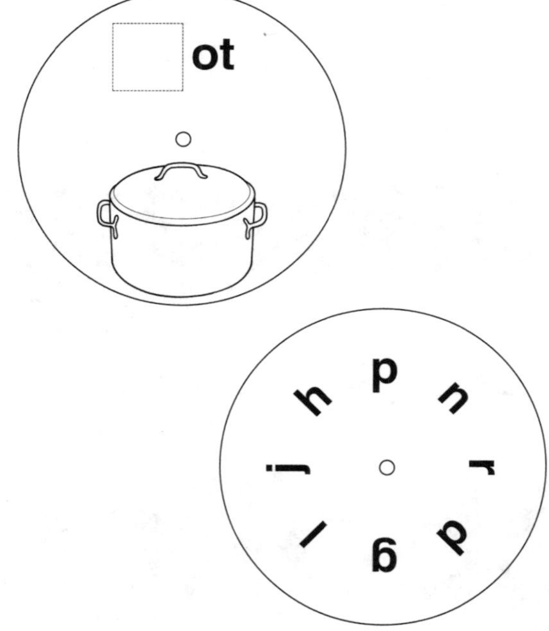

1. Ask the students to cut out the tops and bottoms of their wheels. On each top wheel the students will need to carefully cut out the window surrounded by the dashed lines. (Allow the students to color their wheels if they wish.)
2. Give each student a brad to place in the center of his or her top and bottom wheels. If a wheel does not turn easily, loosen the brad.
3. Have the students turn their center wheels to make as many rhyming words as they can.
4. Tell the students to write all of the words they create on their activity sheets (pages 143 and 144). They may then draw pictures to go along with the words (whenever possible).

Writing Connections

- ✏ Tell the students to use four or more words from their wheels to create poems. They may also illustrate their poetry.
- ✏ Challenge the students to write songs using four or more of the rhyming words. Let them perform their creations for the class, if they desire.

Rhyme Wheels (cont.)

Rhyme Wheels (cont.)

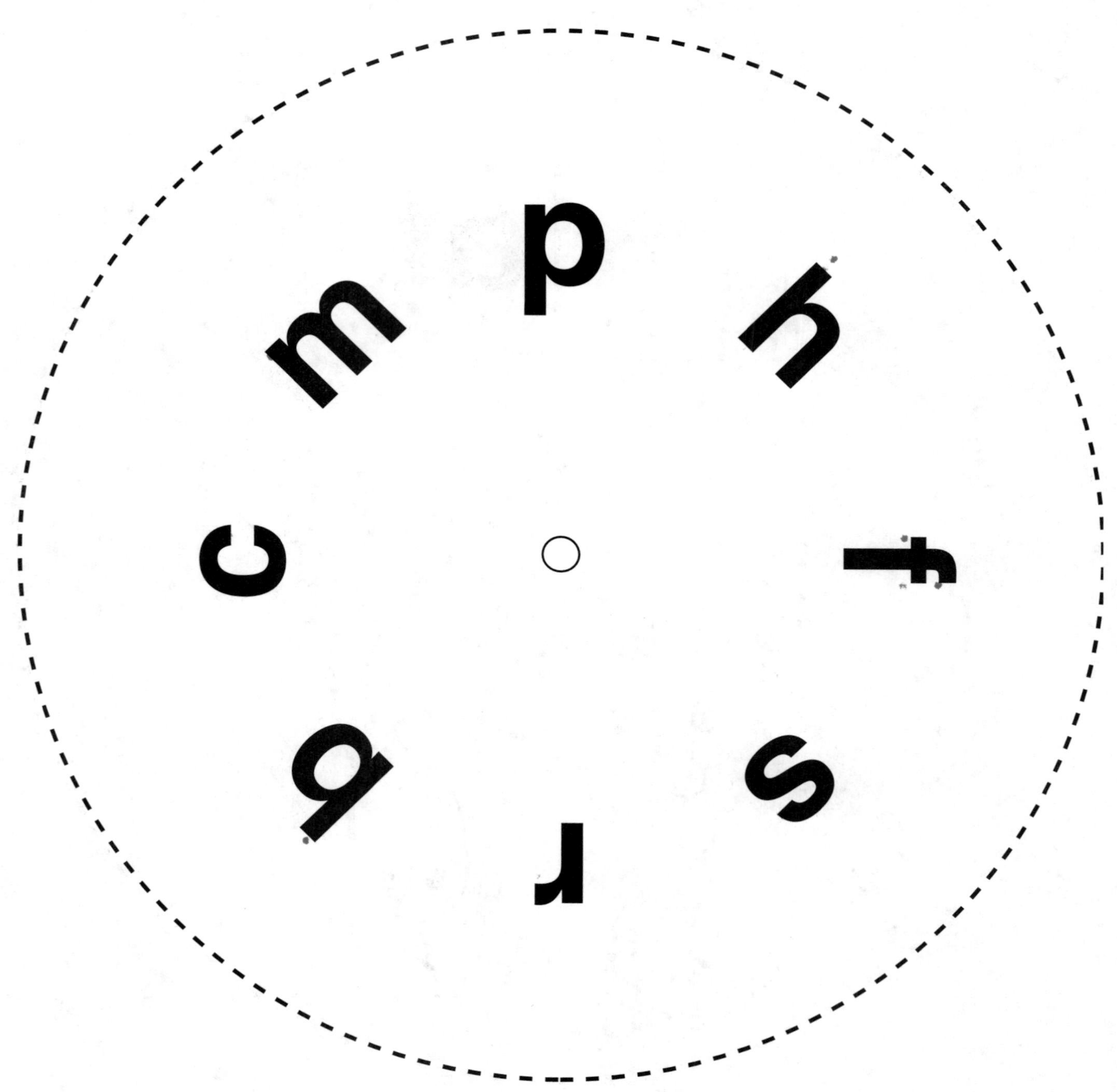

Rhyme Wheels (cont.)

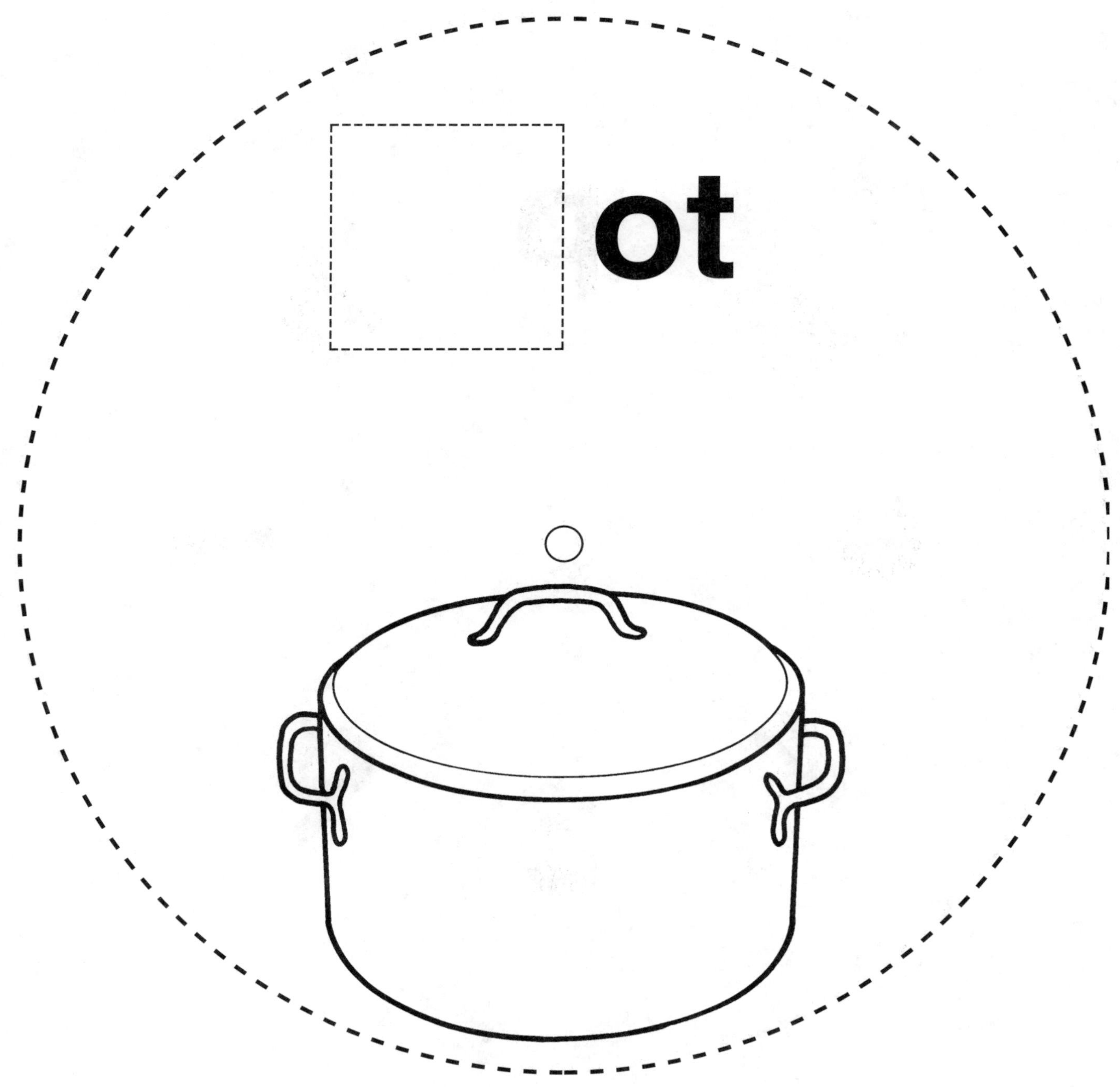

Rhyme Wheels (cont.)

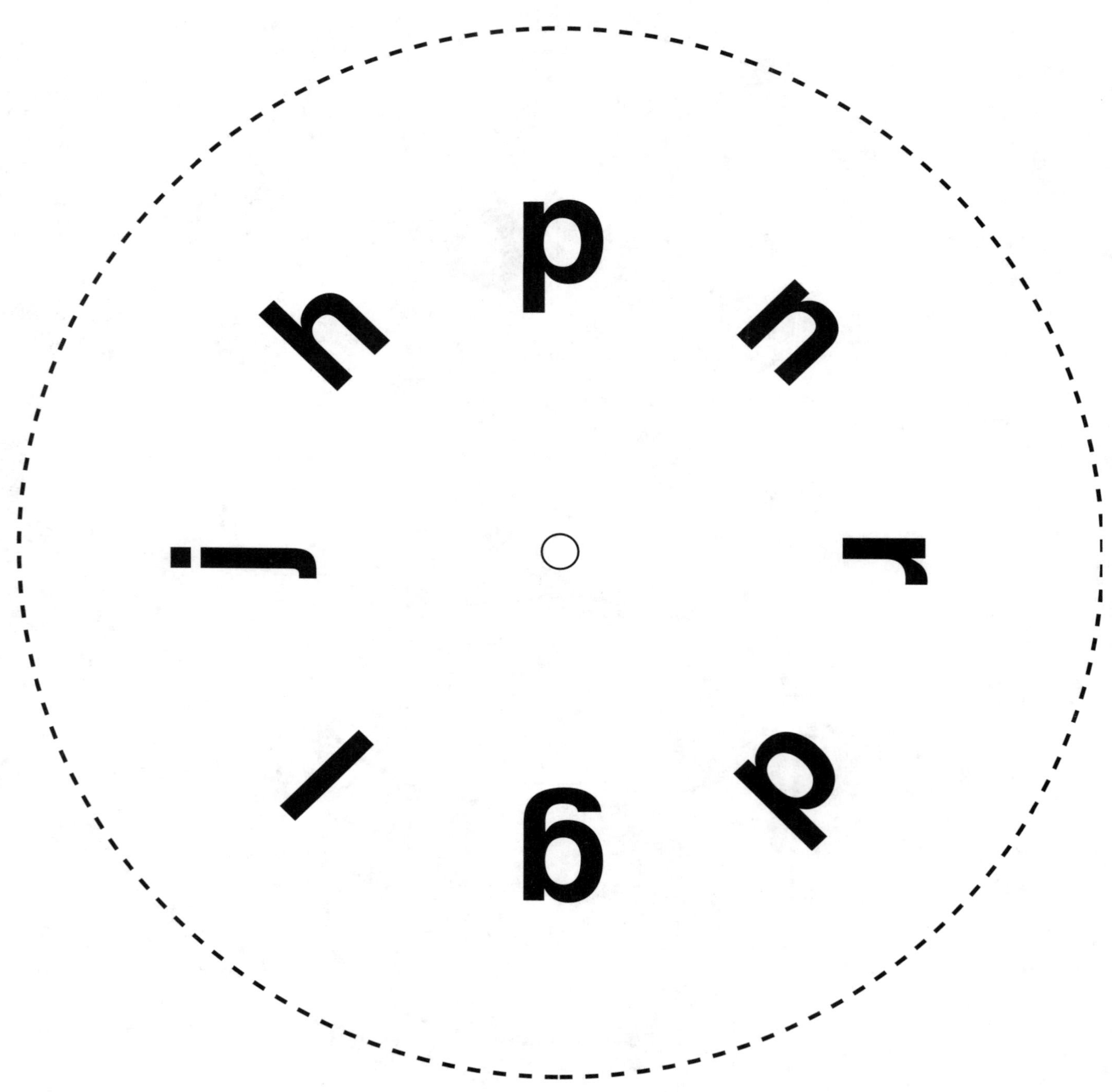

Rhyme Wheels (cont.)

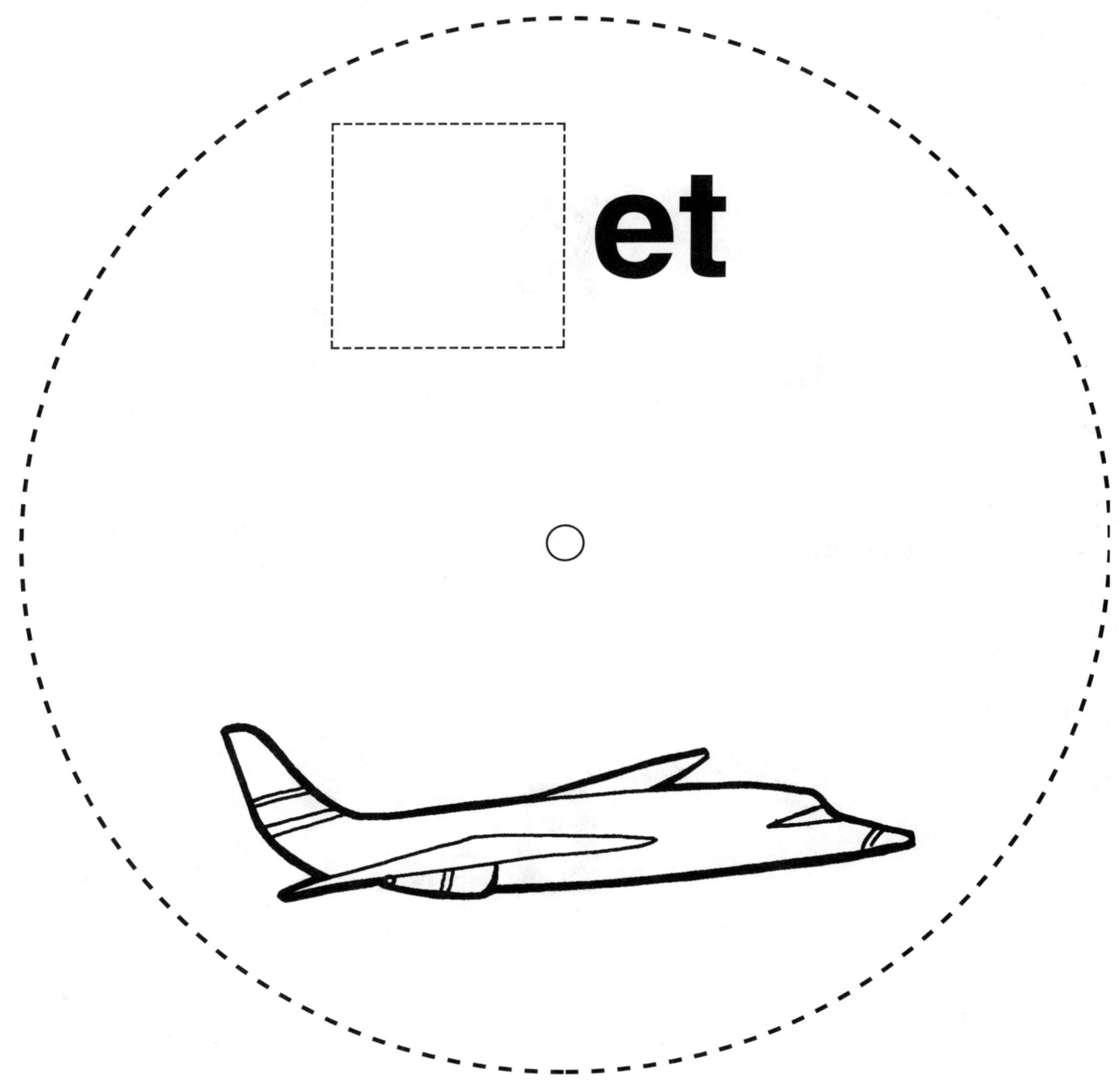

Rhyme Wheels (cont.)

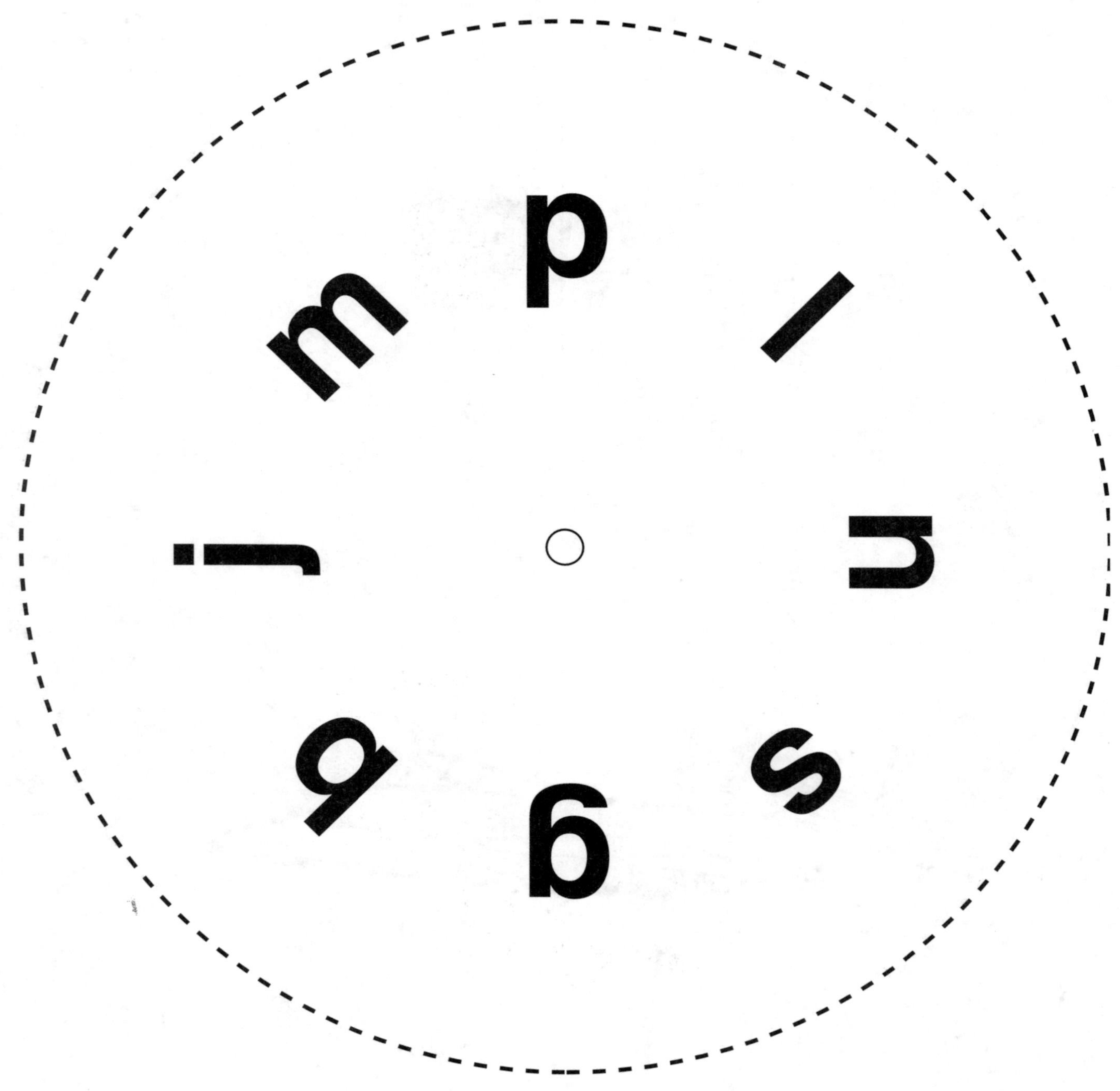

Rhyme Wheels (cont.)

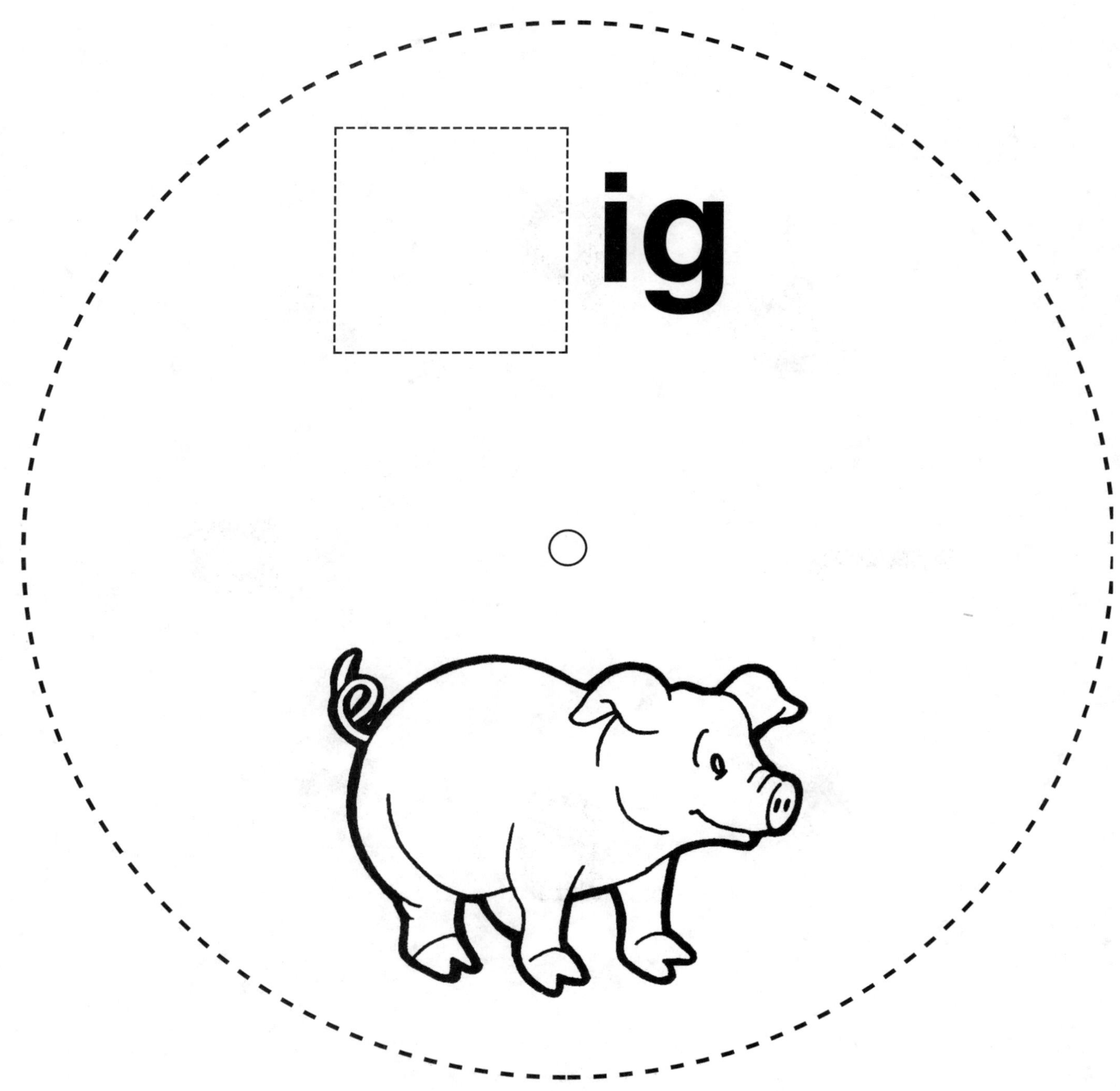

Rhyme Wheels (cont.)

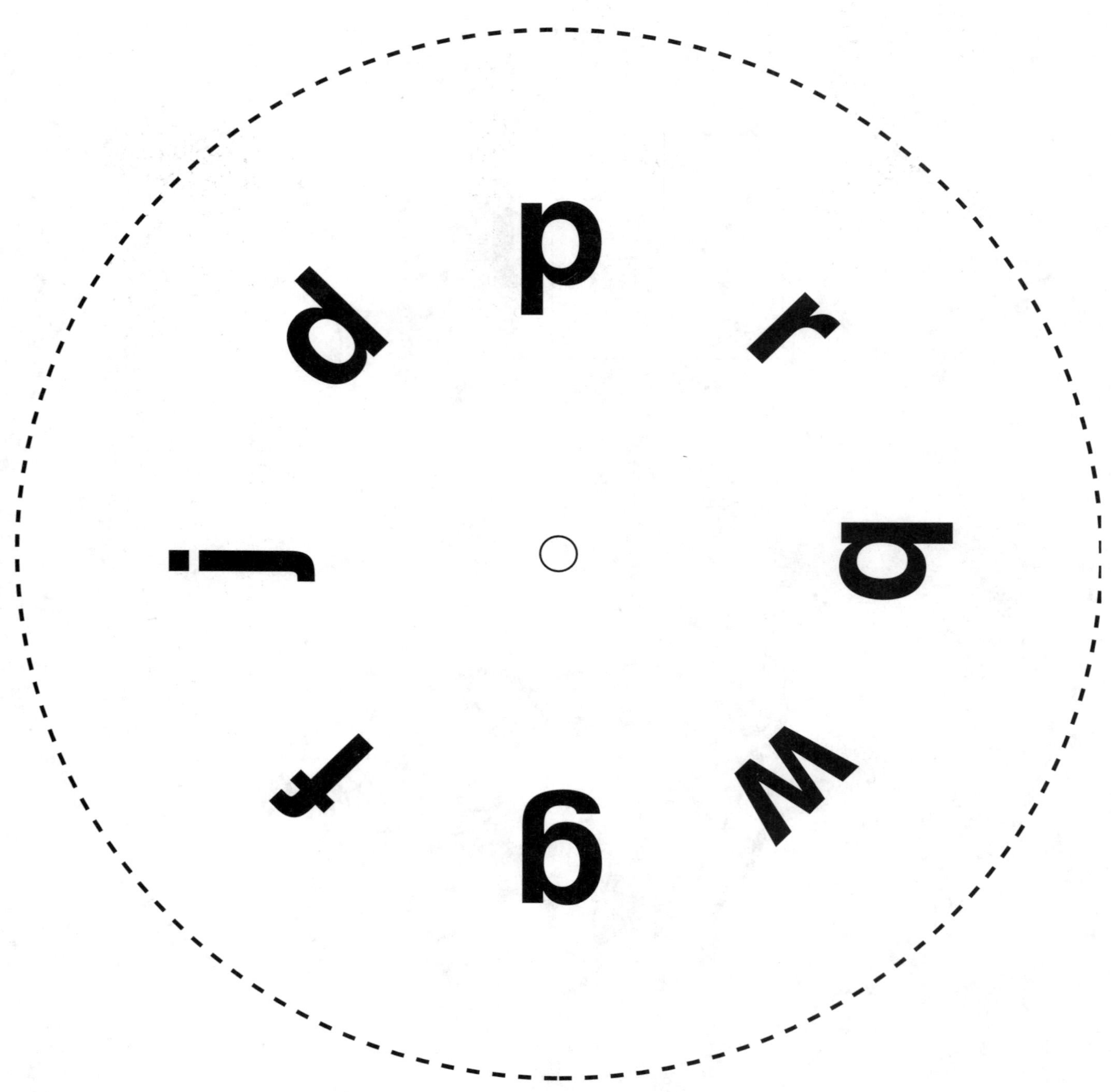

Rhyme Wheels (cont.)

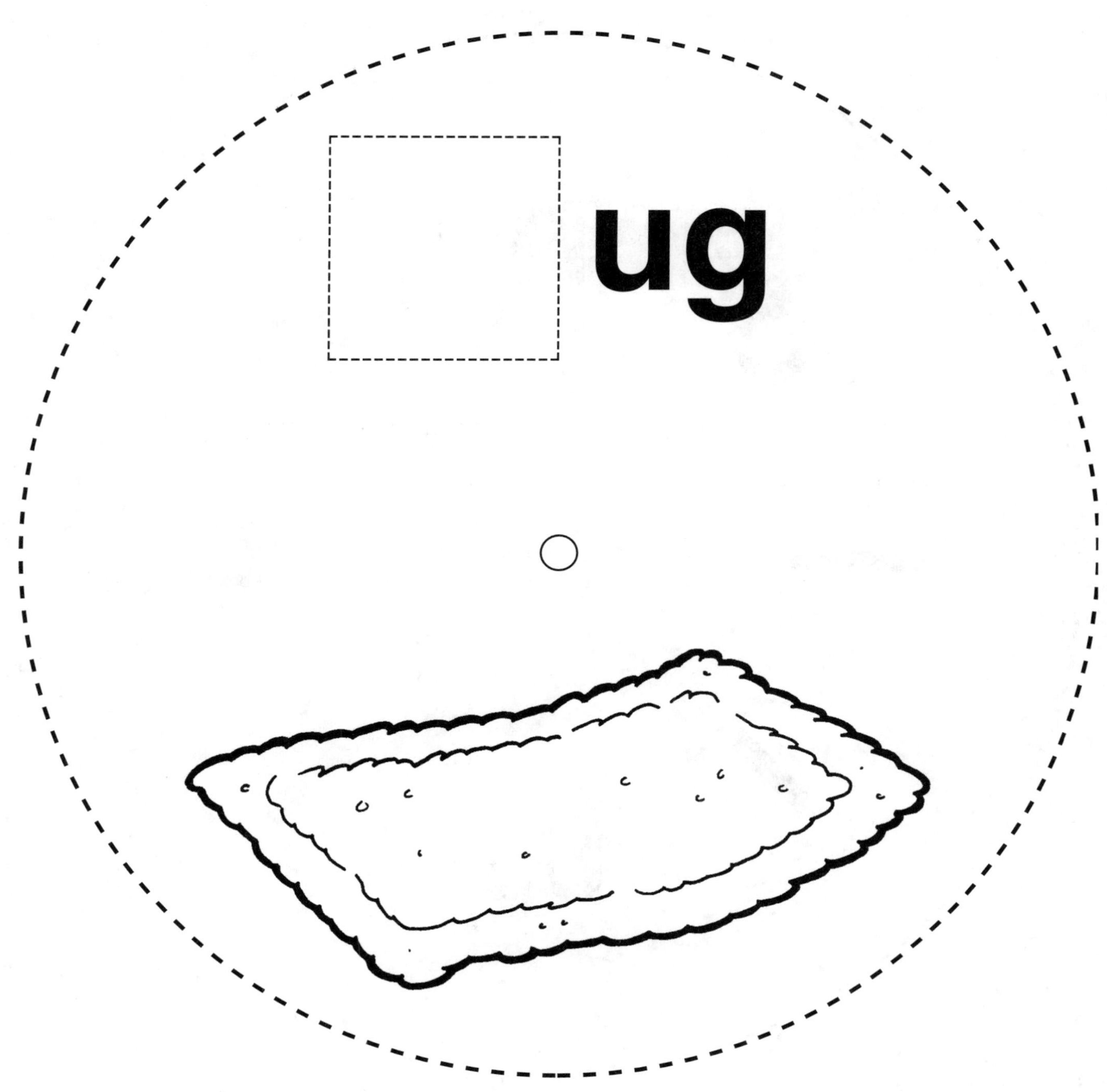

Rhyme Wheels (cont.)

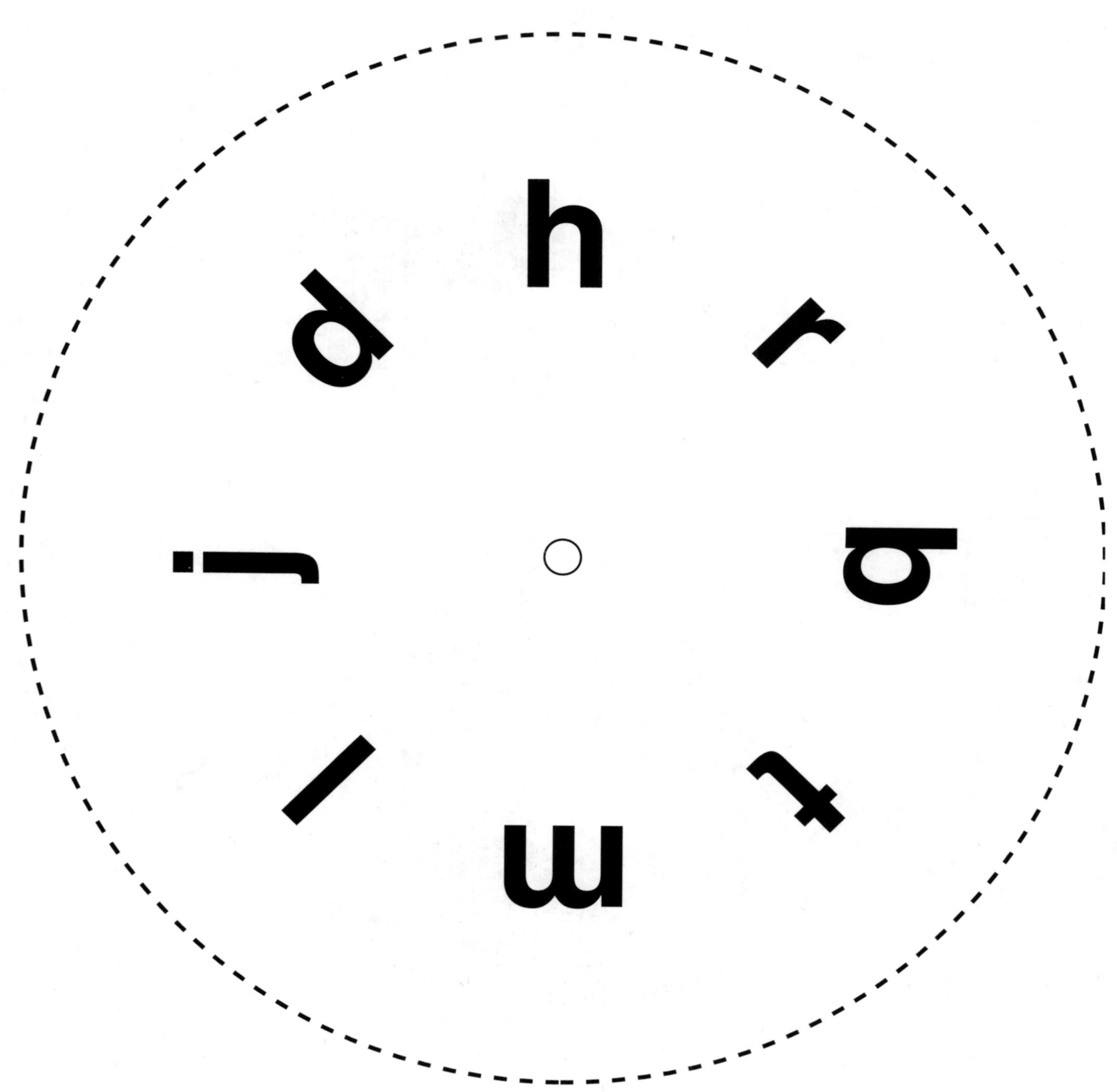

Rhyme Wheels (cont.)

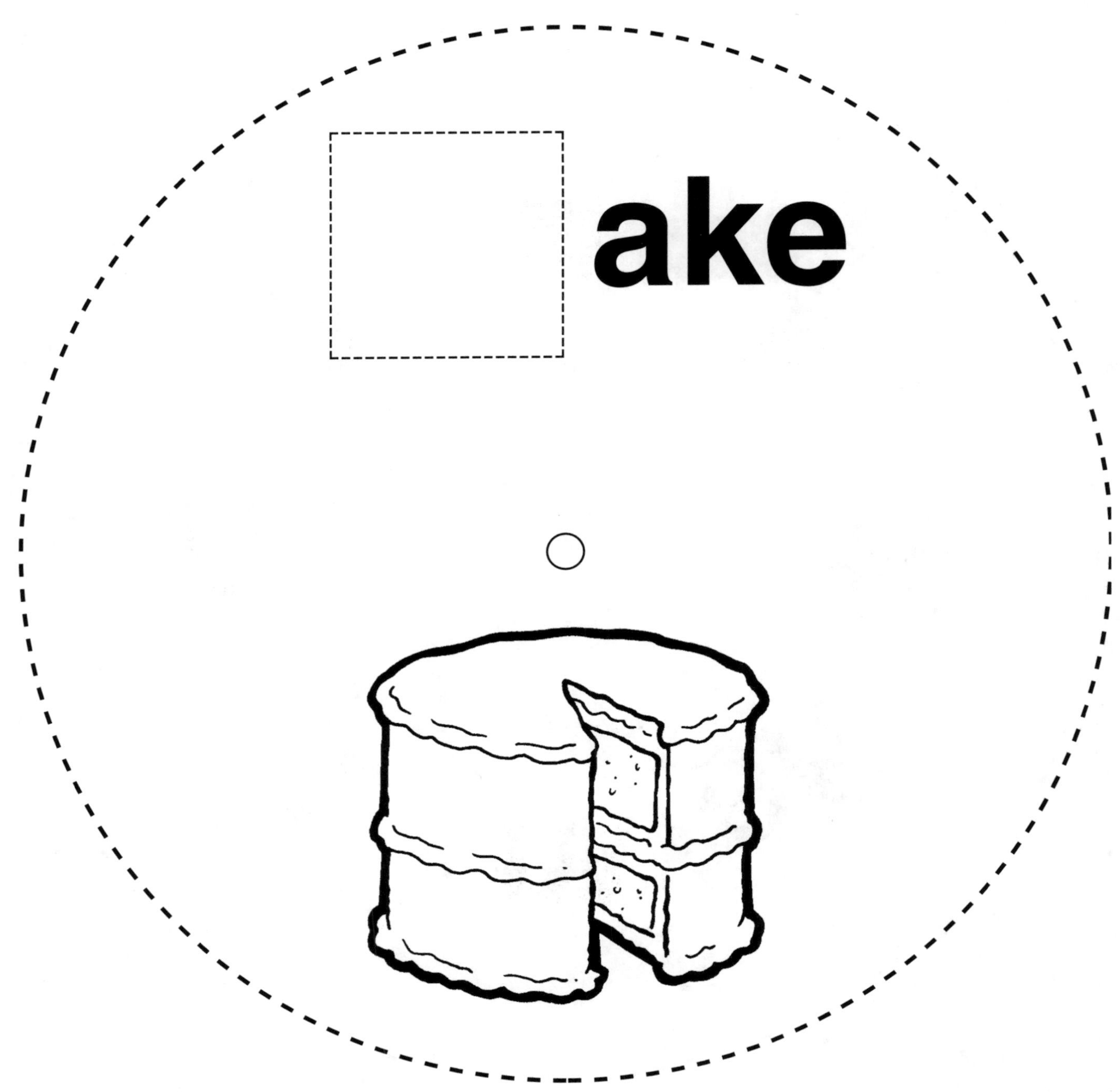

Rhyme Wheels (cont.)

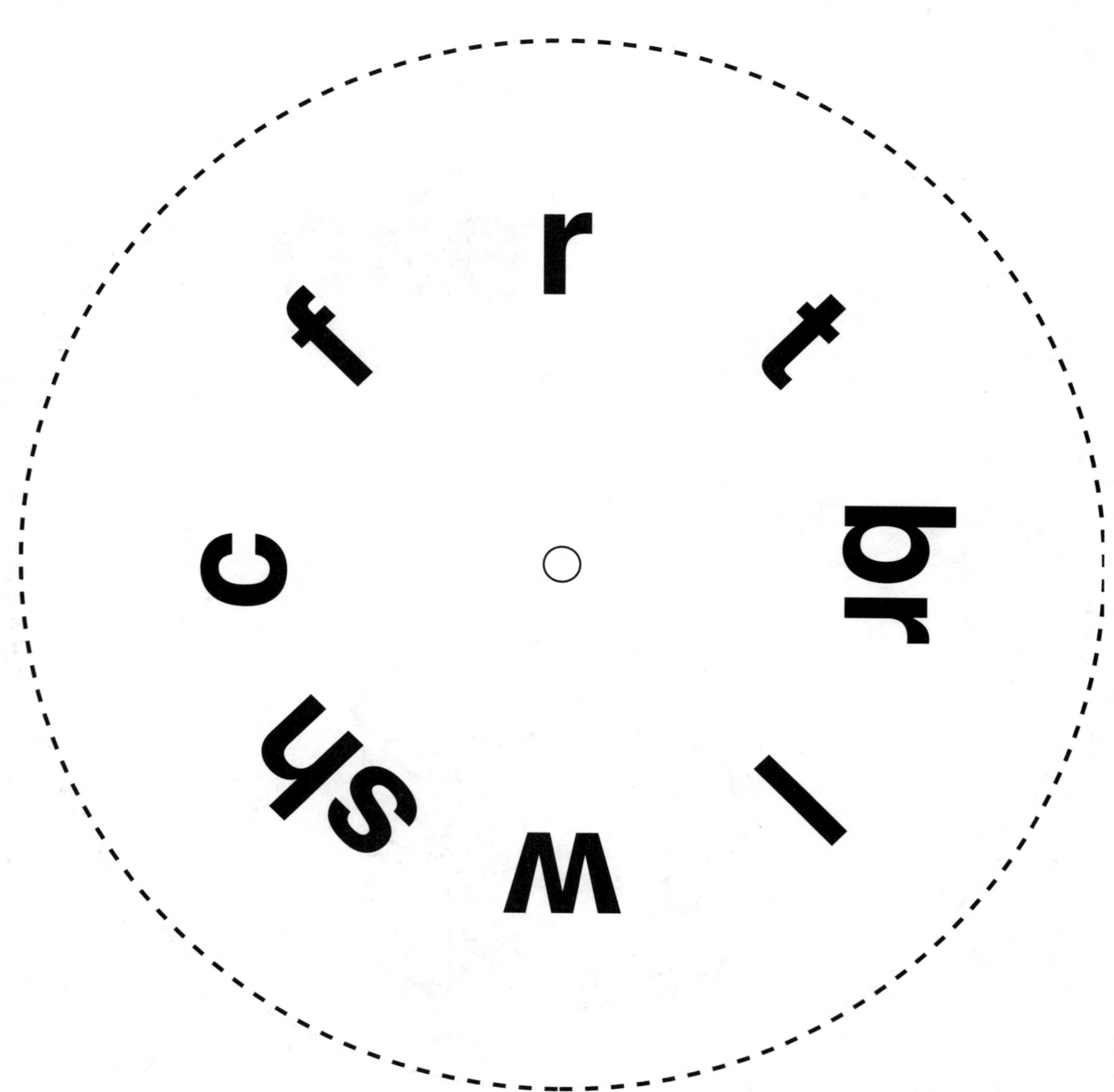

Rhyme Wheels (cont.)

Rhyme Wheels (cont.)

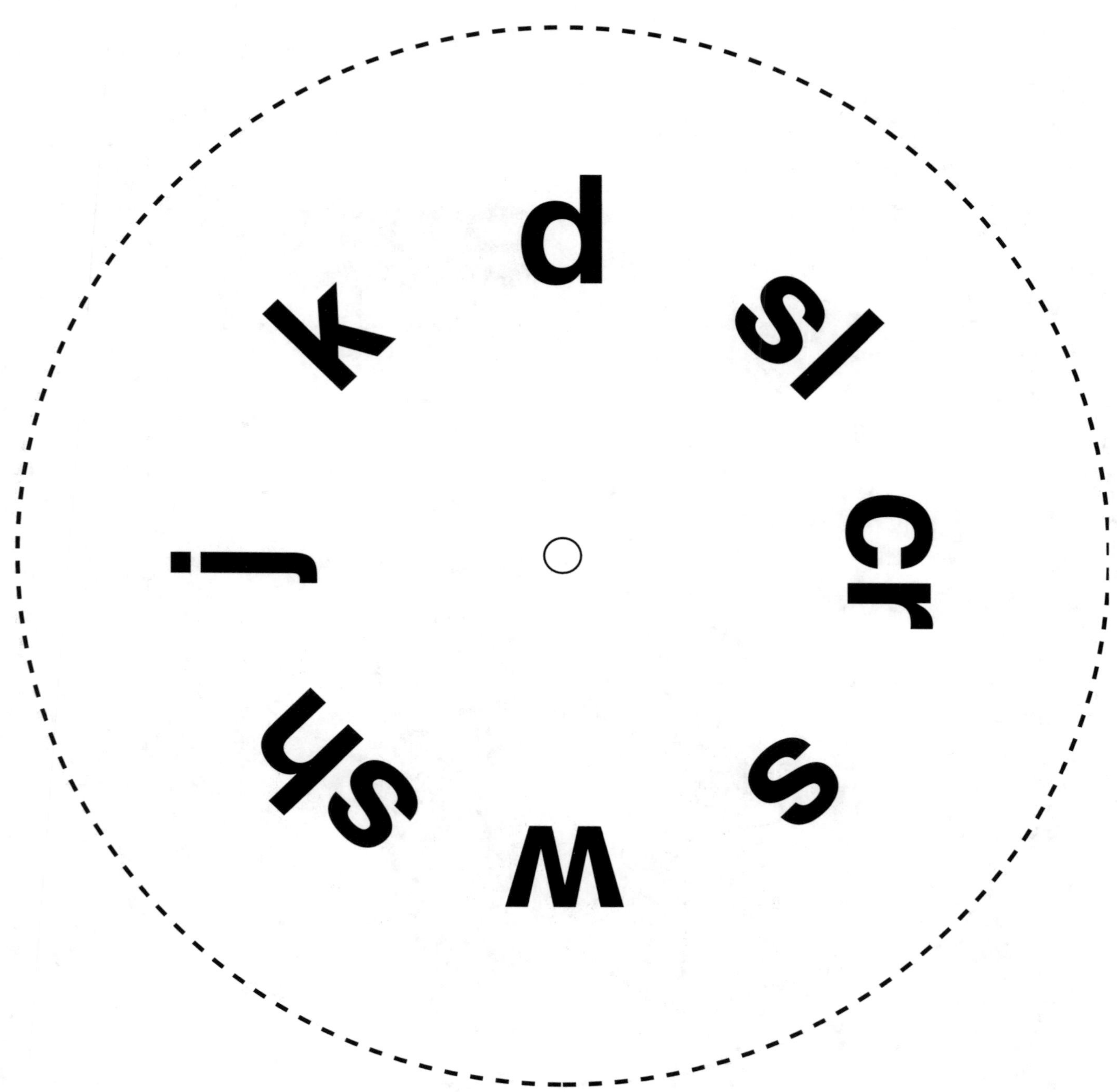

Rhyme Wheels (cont.)

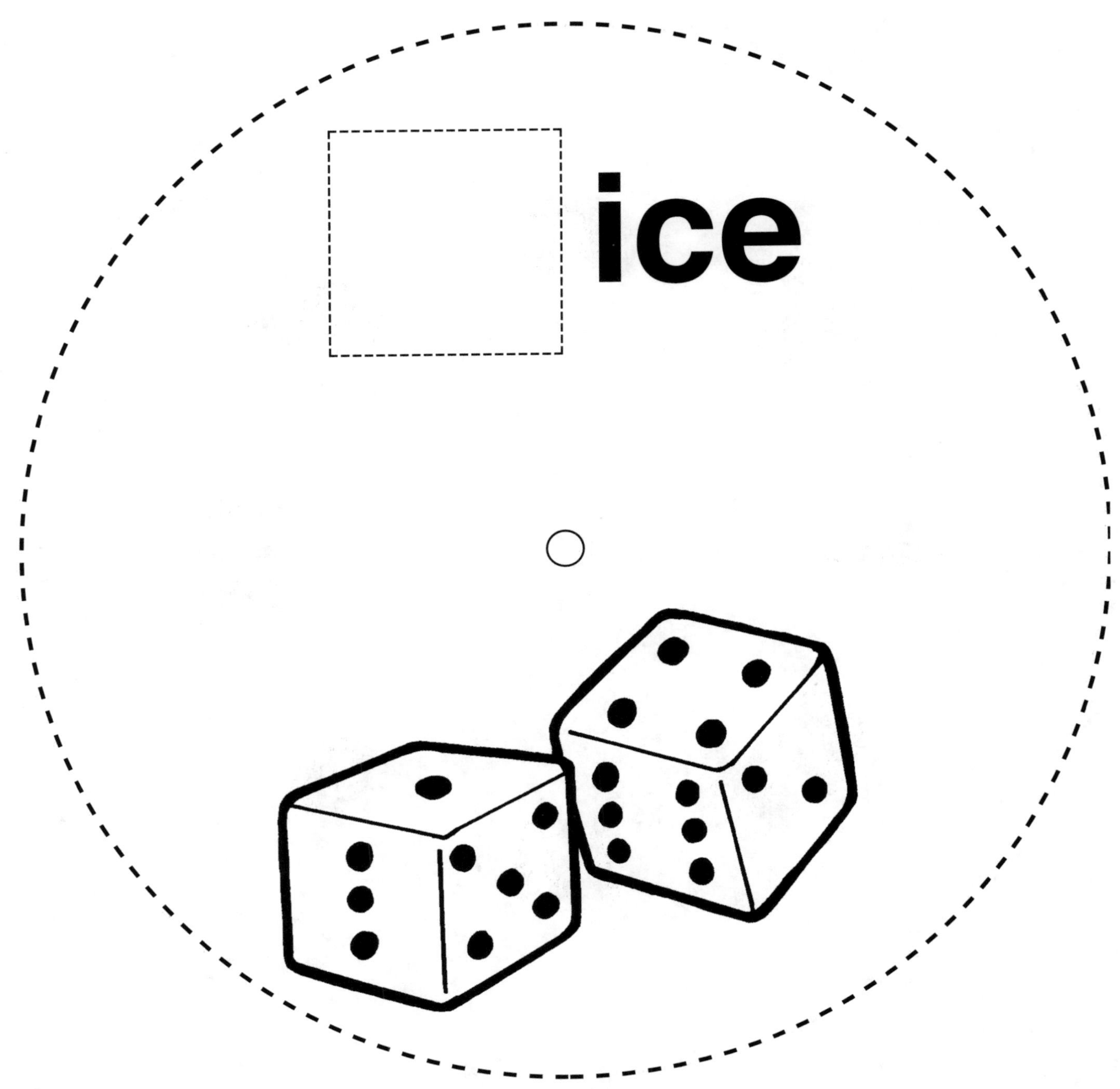

Rhyme Wheels (cont.)

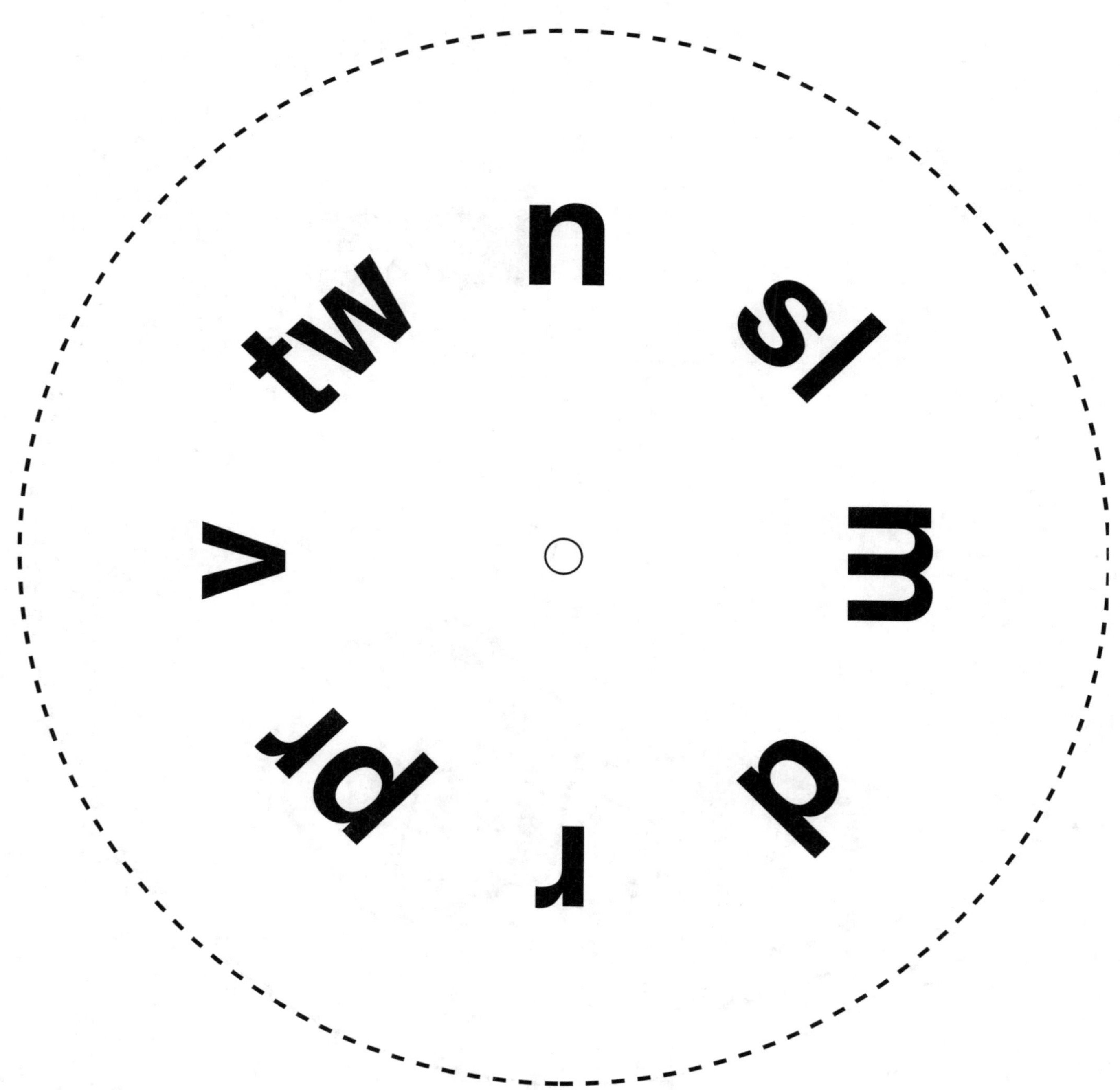

Rhyme Wheels (cont.)

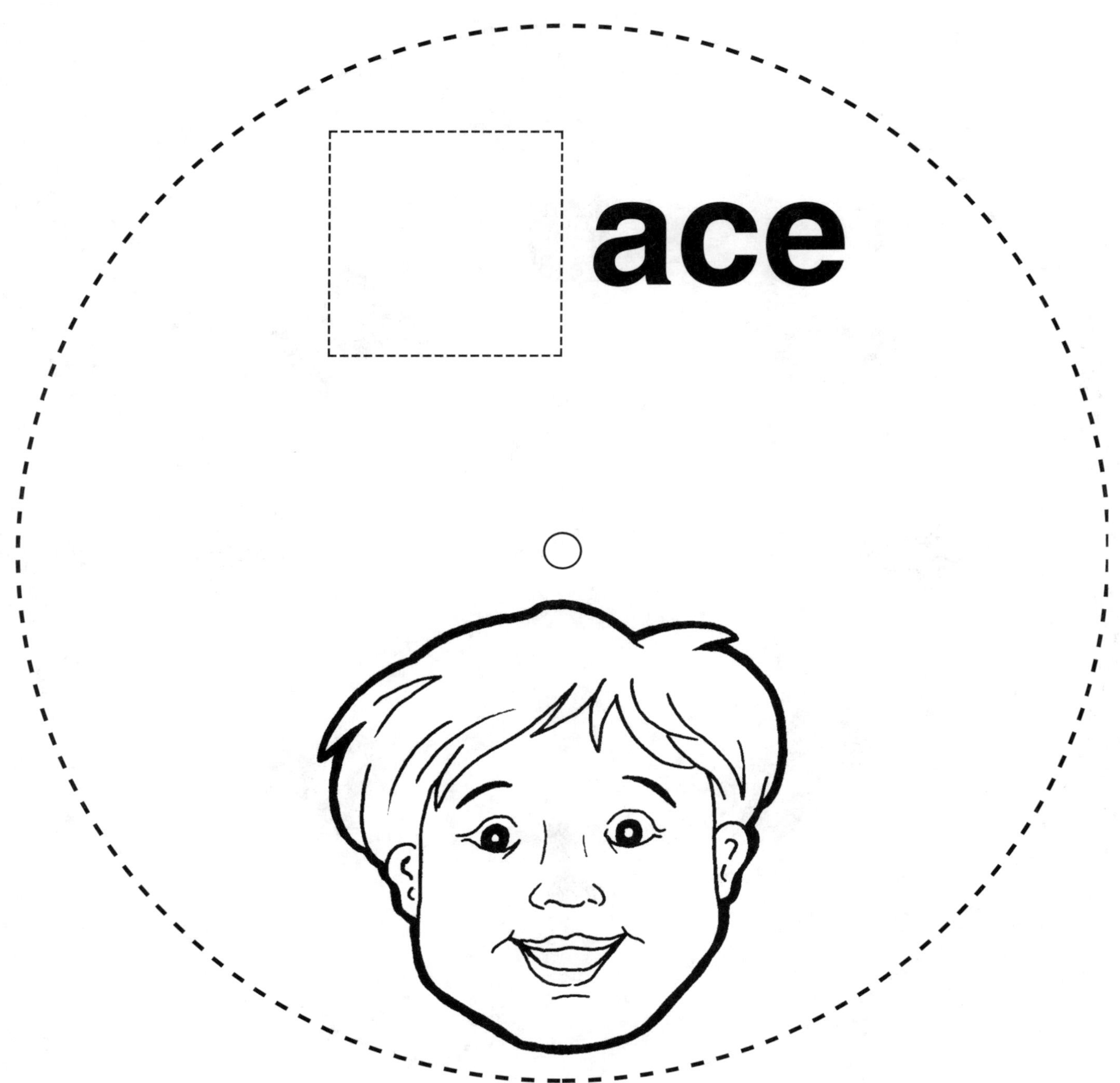

Rhyme Wheels (cont.)

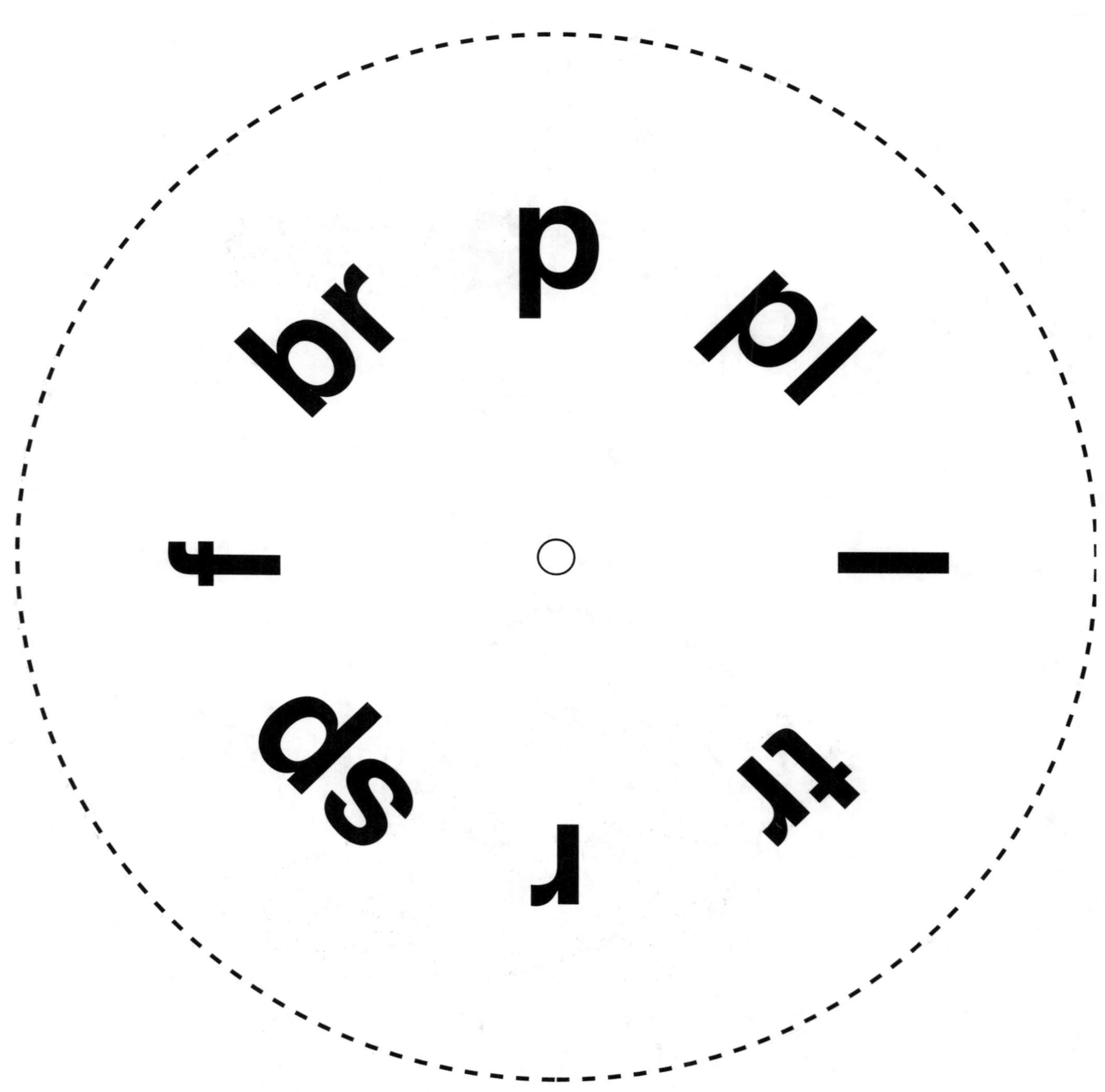

Rhyme Wheels (cont.)

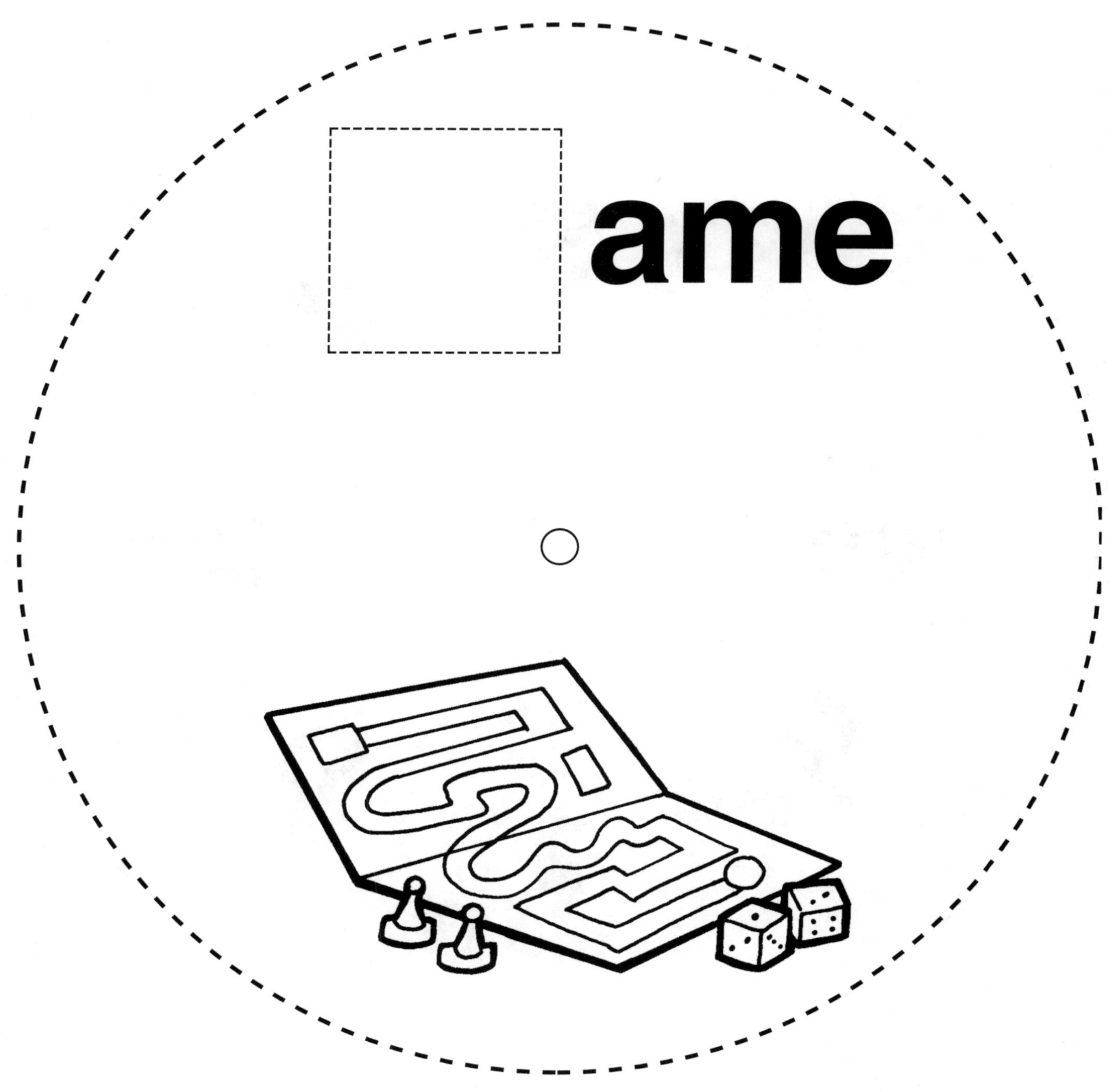

Rhyme Wheels (cont.)

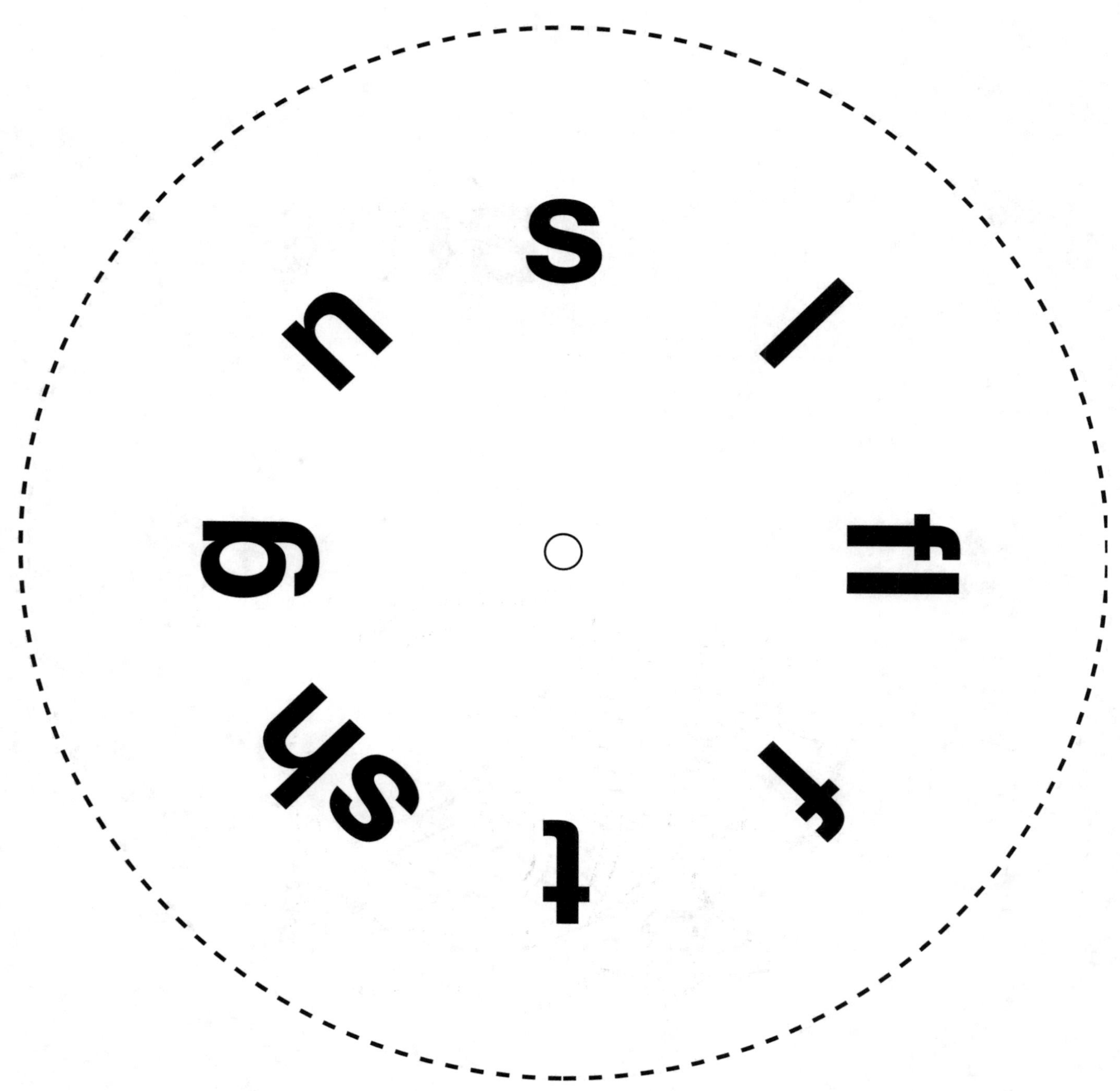

Rhyme Wheels (cont.)

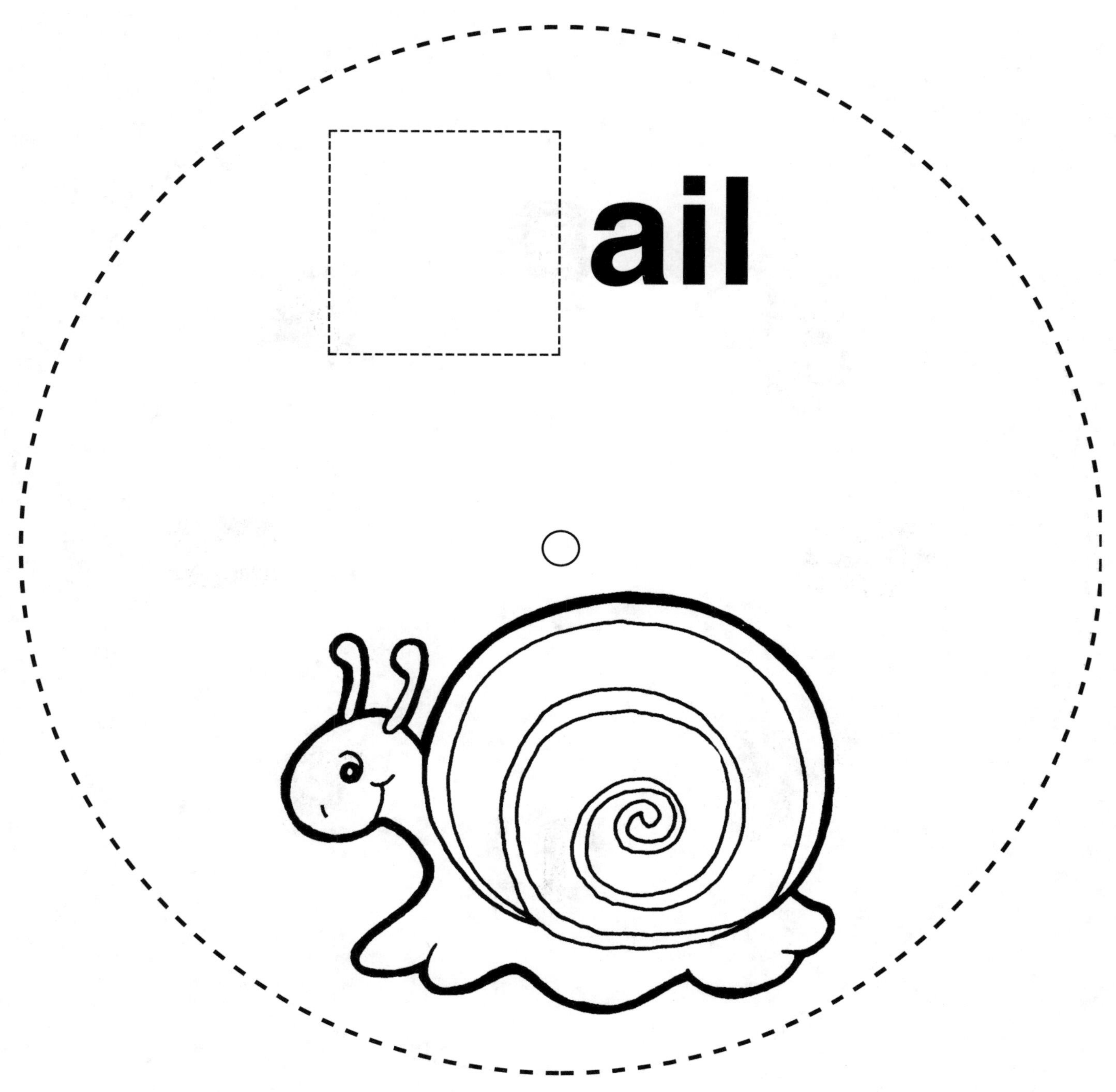

Rhyme Wheels (cont.)